Assessing Mathematical Attainment

Jim Ridgway

NFER-NELSON

62197

*Published by The NFER-NELSON Publishing Company Ltd.,
Darville House, 2 Oxford Road East,
Windsor, Berkshire SL4 1DF, England.*

First published 1988

© *1988, Jim Ridgway*

*Typeset in Times by David John Services Ltd, Slough
Printed by*

*ISBN 0 7005 0680 2
Code 8187 02 1*

Printed in Great Britain by A. Wheaton & Co. Ltd, Exeter

Contents

Preface and Acknowledgements

Mathematical education is currently undergoing much self examination. The nature of the mathematics which should be taught, the way it should be taught, and the way it should be assessed, are all subjects of much debate, and I hope that this book will make a useful contribution to that debate.

My involvement in mathematical education began when I spent two years on secondment at the Shell Centre for Mathematical Education, University of Nottingham. In those days, there was no Cockcroft Report, and wise persons agreed that the 16+ couldn't possibly be introduced before 1990. Things have changed somewhat, but the collaborative work between Nottingham and Lancaster has continued.

Although many of the ideas contained in this volume have grown out of this collaborative work, it would not be helpful to try to identify either the moment of birth or the responsible parent. I can claim though, that the mistakes and silly ideas are all my own.

My thanks are due to Alan Bell, Hugh Burkhardt, Barbara Binns, Rosemary Fraser, John Gillespie, Steve Maddern, Kevin Mansell, Richard Phillips, Andy Pierson, John Pitts, Malcolm Swan, Clare Trott and Di Wharmby for many stimulating discussions. I am particularly grateful to Di Wharmby for the data provided in Appendix 1.

Progress in mathematical education depends heavily on collaborative efforts between teachers, researchers and examiners. I have been fortunate to work with enthusiastic teachers developing classroom materials on topics as varied as the Northern Examining Association Numeracy Scheme, and Advanced Level mechanics. Their ideas and enthusiasm have contributed to my own. In particular, I would like to acknowledge the contributions from Val Aspin, Alan Chisnall, Ray Crayton, Kath Cross, Paul Davison, Mick Fitzgerald, Tansy Hardy, Aidan Harrington, Gill Hatch,

Anne Haworth, Kath Mottram, Mary Robinson, Aileen Stevens, Glenda Taylor, Loraine Waites and Dave Wilson.

Most of the examples contained in this volume are taken from Shell Centre materials. This is not simple parochialism, coupled with ignorance of the valuable work done by others; rather, it is a sort of personal warranty – I have watched all the materials in use in others' classrooms and have used them myself. I am grateful for permission to quote from these materials so extensively. The raw score–standard score conversion table on page 22–3 was reproduced with permission from NFER-NELSON. The extracts from 'Practical Mathematics' by Derek Foxman have been reproduced with the kind permission of the Assessment of Performance Unit.

Several people offered their comments on an early draft of this book; its deficiencies arose because I ignored some of the advice received. However, my thanks are due to Paul Scruton, Phil Levy, Derek Foxman, Chris Whetton, Hugh Burkhardt, Donovan Tagg, Di Wharmby, and Anne Ridgway. Helpful suggestions have also come from NFER-NELSON staff – in particular, from Ian Florance and Lynne McFarland.

Maureen Boots, Dorothy Callis, Tracy Newsham, Sylvia Sumner, Sheila Whalley, and Shealagh Whytock all struggled to produce a decent typescript from muffled dictation and scribbled handwriting. Without their help, the book would not have appeared.

This book, written for teachers, is intended for the well-being of children – in particular for Emma, Rosemary and Alice.

List of Abbreviations

APU	Assessment of Performance Unit
ATM	Association of Teachers of Mathematics
CSE	Certificate of Secondary Education
CSMS	Concepts in Secondary Mathematics and Science Project
DES	Department of Education and Science
GCE	General Certificate of Education
GCSE	General Certificate of Secondary Education
HMI	Her Majesty's Inspectorate of Schools
INSET	In-Service Teacher Education
IQ	Intelligence Quotient
JMB	Joint Matriculation Board
KR-20 and KR-21	Kuder-Richardson Formulae which calculate measures of internal consistency
LEAG	London and East Anglian Group
LFG	The Language of Functions and Graphs
MA	Mathematical Association
MEG	Midlands Examining Group
NCC	National Curriculum Council
NCVQ	National Council for Vocational Qualifications
NEA	Northern Examining Association
NFER	National Foundation for Educational Research
NISEC	Northern Ireland Secondary Examinations Council
PPN	Problems with Patterns and Numbers
PROBS	PRoblem solving OBservation Schedule
SCDC	School Curriculum Development Committee
SCME	Shell Centre for Mathematical Education
SD	Standard Deviation
SEC	Secondary Examinations Council
SEAC	School Examinations and Assessment Council
SEG	Southern Examining Group
SEM	Standard Error of Measurement

TGAT	Task Group on Assessment and Training
TSS	Testing of Strategic Skills
UWHAT	Understanding Without Heavy Acronym Training
WJEC	Welsh Joint Education Committee

Introduction

A great range of tests has been devised to assess mathematical attainment. This range includes formal examinations such as the General Certificate of Secondary Education (GCSE), standardized tests, diagnostic tests, practical tests, records of achievement, end-of-term class tests, and could even include informal classroom discussions. These will soon be joined by national tests, designed to combine the attributes of psychometric tests and ordinary examinations administered at set times in each pupil's educational career, for example, at age 7, 11, 14 and 16 years. Everyone concerned with mathematical education should consider the purposes underlying the administration of any assessment method, the uses to which test results can be put, and the way that both purposes and uses are reflected in the nature of the assessments made. Assessment, the curriculum, and beliefs about the nature of mathematical education are intimately connected. These connections should be to the fore when assessment is considered. Assessment is not something to be done after teaching is finished; assessment techniques must be designed in parallel with teaching, using a common base of conceptions about mathematics, and about the range of skills which pupils should be expected to acquire.

A narrow view of assessment can have a narrowing effect on the curriculum and can lead to a restricted view of mathematics. For example, if scores on standardized tests are revered by Ministers, Local Education Authorities (LEAs), school governors and parents, then teachers will be expected to improve their pupils' scores on such tests. This might lead to a situation in which the school curriculum is shaped by the syllabus implicit in the test items, which also serves as a definition of mathematics, for outsiders. This 'back-wash' effect need not necessarily be a problem, if tests are designed with their likely educational impact in mind (which they rarely are), and are associated with statements about the nature of the abilities being assessed, and offer guidance about how one might use test results to pupils' benefit. However, given the conventional demands that assessment should be neither expensive nor time-consuming, which are likely to rule out practical work, investigation, discussion, problem solving and explanation as activities on which attainment can be assessed, the threat of the likely negative effects of increased use of standardized tests is real enough – despite the claims by the Department of Education and Science that the tests for 7-, 11-, 14-, and 16-year-olds will reflect 'what pupils must achieve to progress in their education and to become thinking and informed people'!

The negative effects of external examinations upon the school curriculum are discussed in Cockcroft (1982). A deliberate attempt is being made to use the GCSE as an instrument for beneficial, examination driven curriculum change. One can only hope that this initiative is successful. This volume contains activities to help individuals and departments to adapt to the new demands likely to be made by GCSE, as part of a general attempt to offer guidance on ways to assess mathematical attainment.

The main goals of this volume and its companion *A Review of Mathematics Tests* are:

* to raise issues about the purposes of assessment;
* to provide information about a variety of types of test, and the match between these and their intended purposes;
* to provide information and guidance on the construction of tests, test administration, and ways that test results might be used in class;
* to describe the GCSE both in general terms and as it relates specifically to mathematics, and to outline the role played by examinations in shaping the processes of mathematical education;
* to describe the National Criteria, and discuss their practical implications;
* to offer ideas for the assessment of topics and processes which have not previously been formally assessed, notably, practical mathematics, problem solving skills, investigative mathematics, and groupwork;
* to help the development within schools of novel assessment tasks which will have a desirable 'back-wash' effect on classroom practices.

Underlying these attempts to offer practical help are a range of purposes which have less tangible aims, but which are at least as important. Some of these are:

* to encourage everyone concerned with mathematical education to consider the role played by the assessment process;

- to improve the quality and range of tests which are available at present;
- to encourage more teachers to set out their own educational aims and objectives, and to develop tests which enable performance to be assessed with respect to these aims and objectives;
- to promote the view that the analysis of tasks and task performance offers a firm basis for discussions about the essential nature of the mathematical endeavour, and can provide a language for communication between teachers and pupils, parents and colleagues;
- to foster the view that both pupils and teachers are part of a large community which shares the common goals of learning about mathematics, about mathematics teaching and learning, and about themselves.

Assessment has not been conceived in a narrow light; as well as standardized mathematics tests, the volume discusses tests of mathematical progress, criterion-referenced tests, and diagnostic tests. It also discusses examinations, including practical tests, tests of mathematical process, and methods of classroom observation. Throughout, emphasis is placed on the uses to which different methods of assessment can be put.

The book is made up of two main sections. The first concerns psychometric tests; how they are designed, constructed, standardized, how they can be evaluated, and how results can be used in class. The second focuses on the GCSE, and the challenges it will pose for assessment and classroom practice. This section describes the new system of examination, and the range of 'missing activities' which must soon be stimulated and assessed in order to satisfy the National Criteria for mathematics.

Guidance is offered on how these new assessment objectives can be attained, beginning with a review of the Testing Strategic Skills project, which adopted many of the assumptions about the need for an examination-driven curriculum that characterizes GCSE. Approaches to stimulating and assessing investigations, problem solving, practical work, groupwork and discussions are described.

By way of review, the penultimate chapter suggests how school mathematics departments can set out to achieve some of their ambitions for mathematics teaching and learning, and how they can begin to meet the new challenges they face. The last chapter offers a unifying framework for the description of assessment and knowledge acquisition by pupils, teachers, examiners and researchers.

Section A

1 Why Use Psychometric Tests?

The introduction of compulsory schooling in Europe and America around the turn of the century led to the development of psychometric tests which attempted to identify those pupils least able to benefit from conventional education. An example of one such test is the Binet Test, produced at the request of the French Government, which was further developed at Stanford University in the USA, where accordingly it became known as the Stanford-Binet Test. Such tests were seen as providing a healthy corrective to previous forms of pupil allocation, based on impressions and subjective judgements, which were shown to be influenced by factors such as the appearance of pupils and their social origins. So the initial impetus for formal testing came from concerns that individuals should receive appropriate education for their abilities, rather than being based on their social background.

The testing movement expanded in a dramatic fashion during and after the First World War. For the first time, tests were published in hundreds of thousands of copies, in the United States at least. One virtue of this development was that scores from a large number of people were made available. Before this, test scores and their interpretation rested on the knowledge and experience of each individual tester. Extensive test score data meant that these intuitive estimates of a candidate's standing relative to (usually) his peers, were replaced by estimates grounded in large-scale data collection.

The early focus of testing on the identification of pupils with special needs, for example, high flyers or low attaining pupils, emphasized different levels of performance and sought to develop tests which accentuated score differences between pupils, with little concern about the underlying causes of these. Work that focused on the detailed analysis of the nature of these performance differences, which might have led to the development of criterion-referenced tests (see page 5) was relatively rare. This development is not too surprising: early test developers could quite reasonably have argued that teachers themselves have clear ideas about the detailed nature of performance in terms of what had been achieved, what remained to be achieved, the relative difficulties of particular topic areas and the like. The early testers' job was to develop tests which cut across such curriculum matters (since schools employ different curricula) to produce tests which could be applied across the entire school population for the purposes of educational screening.

Varieties of tests

The tests industry has grown considerably since its early days. A great variety of tests is now available, made daunting to newcomers by the rich vocabulary which surrounds them. A brief typology is offered here.

Tests of general mental ability aim to assess abilities which are useful in most kinds of thinking. Tests may be referred to as 'Intelligence Tests', which yield 'Intelligence Quotients' (IQs). Conceptions of the nature of intelligence have changed a good deal since early beliefs in a unitary context-free ability. IQs are, perhaps, better thought of in the context of school as 'educational attainment predictors'.

Achievement tests aim to assess attainment in a particular area. Examples might be the ability to understand written French, to design a garden, to dance, or to use algebra. Within this class of tests, *mastery tests* refer to tests designed to establish that a candidate has complete command over a particular set of tasks, and measures of *minimum competency* aim to establish levels of mastery (albeit at rather low levels) which must be attained, for example, before a candidate can gain entrance to a particular profession. (The movement to set tests of literacy and numeracy as entrance barriers to the teaching profession illustrates a possible use for tests of minimum competency.) Several states in the USA set minimum competency tests for pupils.

Aptitude tests are intended to predict later performance. For example, aptitude tests may be used to identify people who will complete training courses successfully or whose job performance is likely to be high. An employer might set a collection of tests – an aptitude test battery – to select people for employment. Such tests need not be different in kind to any other sort of test. It is only their use which allows us to describe them as aptitude tests. All tests are achievement tests in so far as they report on the development and learning of individuals up to the point at which the test is taken; any test can be seen as an aptitude test if it is used to predict future performance of any sort.

Norms, criteria and diagnosis

In the context of mathematical education, the three commonest kinds of tests are: *norm-referenced tests*; *criterion-referenced tests*; and *diagnostic tests*.

Norm-referenced tests report where a pupil stands in comparison with other pupils who have taken the same test.

Criterion-referenced tests set out to judge whether or not a pupil has been able to perform some well-defined task to an acceptable standard. Full criterion-referencing requires a complete statement to be made about each aspect of the tasks to be performed and the level of competence required. The intention is to define tasks in an unambiguous way so that pupils, teachers, parents and employers can be clear about what has been achieved. A statement such as, 'can stay afloat for two minutes without assistance, without touching the sides or bottom of a swimming pool', is a criterion which most people can make a judgement about with a reasonable degree of consensus. So too is, 'can read 12-point upper-case letters at twelve inches'. Whereas a statement such as, 'can swim 200 metres unaided' and 'reads well without glasses' are, by the standards of full criterion-referencing, rather ambiguous criteria, since neither task is completely specified. (This is illustrated by the Amateur Swimming Association, whose certificates of swimming competence issue warnings that the certificate holders should not expect to perform as well in cold or rough water as they can in warm swimming pools.)

The problems of defining the 'National Criteria for Mathematics' are considered in a later chapter *Examining the National Criteria* (pages 71–76). Briefly, it can be noted that expressions such as 'understands' or 'forms generalizations' are far too ill-defined to be considered 'criteria' in the sense implied by criterion-referenced tests.

Diagnostic tests set out to identify pupil conceptions and misconceptions so that appropriate remedial action may be taken.

Different conclusions can be drawn from these different forms of test. Suppose that three versions of a test called *Measurements* were developed. Pupil performance could be reported as follows: *norm-*

referenced – Anne scored more marks on *Measurements* than 75 per cent of a large national sample of 15-year-olds, Jim had a standard score between 40 and 50; *criterion-referenced* – Anne can use her handspan to measure classroom furniture with errors of 10 per cent or less, she can measure the volume of irregularly shaped small objects via immersion in water, Jim can use a stopwatch to time sporting events, to an accuracy of two seconds; *diagnostic* – Anne has attained Level 4 understanding on the *Measurements* test. She demonstrates mastery of the techniques and exhibits no obvious conceptual misunderstandings, Jim has problems with origins, and when estimating distances on a map, he omits the interval 0–1 from the scale, and when using a measure of, say, five miles, measures from units 1 to 5 on the scale provided; when finding the volume of a 4 x 4 x 4 block of cubes, he calculates 4 x 3 x 3 ('so that the same block isn't counted three times').

These three uses are conceptually distinct. Test designers also embark on different methods of test development when they set out to produce tests of each type. For example, the development of diagnostic tests usually begins with detailed interviews of a large number of pupils, in a search for common misconceptions; the development of norm-referenced tests should involve large scale testing of pupils representative of the school population as a whole. Nevertheless, any test can be used to produce any kind of interpretation. The key issue is the purpose of testing, and the way the test is used.

Purposes of testing

Norm-referencing, criterion-referencing, and diagnosis, have different purposes. These can be itemized as follows.

NORM-REFERENCING

1. Comparison with a standardizing sample, for the purposes of evaluating school performance with respect to a 'national standard'.
2. Making comparisons between schools, or between different educational treatments.
3. Comparing the effectiveness of different teachers by examining relative pupil gains after each year's teaching (or within school years, on parallel classes).
4. Rank ordering pupils for the purposes of: identifying children

who are markedly under-performing (so that remedial action can be taken); identifying pupils of high attainment for whom more elaborate challenges might be provided; grouping children (either into streams, or into mixed ability classes).
5. Following pupil progress over time.
6. Taking account of differences in age when pupils are compared, since each pupil's standard score is based on a comparison with peers in the same narrow age band (say one month), rather than with the whole year group.

Of course, purposes 1, 2 and 3 involve considerations other than just test scores. For example, an evaluation of school performance would require some clear understanding about educational intentions, considerations of syllabus and curricular matters, knowledge about the catchment area, and so on. Such conceptual issues take more to resolve them than the administration of single, simple, measures!

CRITERION-REFERENCING

1. Purposes 1–5 under norm-referencing can often be satisfied by criterion-referenced tests.
2. Specifying the nature of what has, and has not been attained.
3. Identifying particular strengths and weaknesses of individual pupils, which can form the basis for personal work plans.
4. Identifying class strengths and weaknesses, to highlight topics which need more, and perhaps different, teaching effort.
5. Forming the basis for discussions with pupils, parents and colleagues.
6. Forming the basis for a dialogue about curricular matters as well as about pupil performance, at transition points such as changes in class, or changes of schools.

DIAGNOSTIC TESTING

1. All the purposes under criterion-referencing can often be satisfied by diagnostic tests.
2. Identifying specific pupil misconceptions which underlie particular errors (and sometimes describing teaching strategies to overcome these errors).
3. Describing hierarchies of conceptual development which have implications for teaching.

Which kind of test is best?

These brief descriptions might be taken to suggest that one should always choose to use a diagnostic test, since it might well serve most of the purposes fulfilled by norm- and criterion-referenced tests. Of course, the choice is not so simple. The virtues of diagnostic tests are bought at the cost of breadth of coverage. A 40 minute diagnostic test is likely to cover a narrow domain, such as fractions or vectors. A norm-referenced test is likely to attempt a much wider sampling across domains within the same time limit. This can be illustrated by comparing the content of any one of the *Chelsea Diagnostic Tests* with, say, the Senior form of the *Graded Mathematics-Arithmetic Test* in the Summary Table of *A Review of Mathematics Tests* (Ridgway, 1988a).

2 The Design and Evaluation of Standardized Tests

A standardized test is one in which the procedure for test administration, the test content, equipment, and resources to be used, together with the scoring scheme, have all been set out in such a way that precisely the same testing procedures can be followed at different times and places by different testers and examinees. Tests are sometimes wrongly described as being 'standardized' simply because the test publisher has presented data on test scores from a large sample of people. It is clear that data on scores (called 'test score norms') can be provided for unstandardized tests, and that standardized tests can be presented without norms. There is little point in collecting norms for unstandardized tests. The value of collecting norms for standardized tests depends to a great extent on the way the scores were collected, and on the uses to which the test scores are to be put. (Confusion is added by the term 'standardized score'. This refers to a particular statistical technique for reporting scores, and says nothing about how these scores were derived.)

Tests can vary a good deal in their objectivity. For an objective test the guidelines for the assessment of performance are laid down explicitly, and different judges should arrive at very similar answers. Some tests allow a good deal of discretion on the part of the marker, thus increasing their subjective component, as in essay marking.

For the purposes of this discussion, the term 'standardized test' will refer to a test prepared for standardized administration, for which rules for scoring are available, and for which test score norms have been prepared.

This chapter describes some of the technical and conceptual issues involved in the design of tests, in order to demystify the processes of test construction. Guidance is offered on ways to judge tests and test manuals, and on how to use them in class.

Test development

The first stage in test design is to decide on the pupils for whom the test is intended (in terms of pupil age, or past attainment, for example) and on the mathematical content of the test.

Defining the pupil target group

Information about the age range of the pupils for whom the test is designed can usually be found in the test manual. Discovering the actual age range of pupils who took part in the standardization exercise often needs some detective work, however. It is clear that the presentation of normative data for groups outside the age range of the pupils actually tested makes the strong assumption that scores can be extrapolated. The greater the discrepancy between the age range of the group actually tested and the target group, the greater the scope for errors of interpretation. Another issue is the school year of the standardizing group, which has been shown to affect pupil performance. Scores obtained from junior school pupils aged 11 years may not be an appropriate base from which to judge the performance of pupils of the same age in middle schools or secondary schools.

Descriptions of test items

Test content should always be a prime concern of test designers and test users. A danger associated with over-use of standardized tests of achievement is that they can have an unfortunate effect on the kind of education which children receive. If scores on standard attainment tests are revered by LEAs, school governors and parents, then there will be pressure on teachers for their pupils to score highly on such tests. This can lead to an undesirable 'back-wash' effect in which the school curriculum is shaped by the syllabus implied in the test items. This need not be a problem if the tests had been carefully designed with a view to their educational impact, and if care was taken about the choice of tests in terms of test content.
     One might reasonably expect test authors to provide information about the rationale which underlies their choice of test items. They might be expected to define the rules for item construction, and to provide some idea of which features of each test item increase or decrease the difficulty of that item, and to give information about

the universe of problems to which success on this item is likely to generalize. Detailed descriptions of how test items were constructed are very rare in test manuals. Another serious deficiency of many tests is that test authors fail to provide an overall description of the coverage of the test items in their tests; domains are ill-specified, as are the processes which pupils are required to engage in within those domains. Test manuals should provide a test blueprint which describes the composition of the test, and which reflects the spread of items devoted to particular domains and processes.

Failure to provide any rationale for the particular choice of test items or any description of test content, can have strong negative pedagogical implications. Consider, for example, the *Y Mathematics Series*. These tests supposedly measure 'mathematical understanding over a wide range of concepts and situations' yet the items in *Y1* focus almost entirely on arithmetic operations on multiple digit numbers. The author seeks to reassure the user that details of test content 'should not...be a matter for fundamental concern' because pupils who do well on arithmetic also do well on other mathematical challenges.

There is a considerable danger in presenting teachers with a view that mathematical attainment in the first few years in primary school is best assessed by examining performance solely on the four basic operations of addition, subtraction, multiplication, and division. A number of tasks face the teacher of mathematics. Helping pupils to master skills is an obvious task. Less obvious is the job of alerting pupils to the beauty of mathematics; to the joys of discovery, and to the excitement of finding regularities in the world around them. One of the problems in mathematical education is that primary school teachers of mathematics have often had little mathematical training themselves, and indeed may not have experienced the beauty, joy and excitement of mathematics as pupils. Teaching these aspects of mathematics requires both considerable skill and a good deal of confidence. Presenting teachers with a notional 'national standard' of mathematical ability, which relates only to basic number skills is a rather negative thing to do, since it implicitly denies the relevance of other useful mathematical activities.

Any test which purports to measure mathematical attainment without providing operational definitions of what has been attained is of limited use, since the scope for subsequent action is severely reduced. Suppose an ill-defined test of 'mathematical attainment' is given to a class, and the teacher discovers that the class is performing well below the norms set out in the manual. How might the teacher respond? The teacher can 'try harder', or might try to rationalize the results on the following grounds: that the normative data are atypical; that these children are less able; that the class had an 'off-day', and so on. Nothing in the manual or the test items provides the basis for teachers to reappraise their own teaching, or to help the pupils increase their skills.

Conversely, when test manuals analyse the nature of the mathematical operations to be performed, and describe the contexts in which these operations are embedded (measuring rooms, cutting cakes, weighing things), far more can be done. A discussion of how items were constructed lends itself naturally to the development of the test as a diagnostic instrument for both teacher and pupil use. If the whole class has difficulty with a certain type of problem, there are strong reasons to suppose that they have either had inadequate practice on problems of this sort, or that they have been inadequately taught (the item may well, of course, face pupils with particularly difficult challenges).

The teacher can respond by reviewing current approaches to the teaching of this particular topic; reanalysing the ways it has been taught, and looking for different approaches. There are many sources of new ideas – notably colleagues at school, and publications such as *Mathematics Teaching* and *The Mathematical Gazette*. Regular self-appraisal is essential for the skill growth of both teachers and pupils; test results which are based on some clear task specification can provide a good basis for this self-appraisal and remediation. Discussion of the rules for constructing items should allow the teacher to develop worksheets graded by difficulty level to facilitate learning, and to provide the basis for subsequent testing to evaluate the effects of the redesigned lessons.

When the performance of a particular pupil is considered, discussion of the nature of the mathematical operations assessed will provide strong clues about remedial (or indeed new) teaching, which will improve the overall performance of the individual. This has obvious relevance for the immediate task of helping a particular pupil; it can also have longer term benefits for the teacher. A detailed analysis of any small mathematical domain is likely to highlight pupil misconceptions which had heretofore gone unnoticed by the teacher. Describing, assessing and remediating these misconceptions can have a generally beneficial effect on teacher skills, transferable to interaction with other pupils, once one has been sensitized to particular patterns of misconceptions. So detailed descriptions of tasks and common errors can build up teachers' knowledge of pupils' problems and offer some pointers to remediation – thus offering the possibility of personal skill development for both teachers and pupils.

In the absence of a test blueprint (and sometimes in its presence) the user must decide what the test assesses. This requires the content of each test item to be related to some conceptual framework for classifying mathematical tasks. A number of such frameworks exist, or are implicit in documents such as *Mathematics Counts* or *Mathematics 5–16* (Her Majesty's Inspectorate of Schools, 1985). The illustration provided here is taken from *A Review of Mathematics Tests* (Ridgway, 1988a). It is offered as a stimulus for personal reflection, rather than as a definitive system to be used without modification. An attempt was made to make judgements about content validity and to categorize test content in tabular form, in order to give test users an impression of the different balances of test content chosen by different test authors. Items were classified in terms of Domain (Number, Measurement, Space, Algebra, Logic, and Statistics) and the Process required (Recall, Technique, or Comprehension). They were also categorized as being set in a concrete context, or posed as abstract problems. Throughout, an effort was made to judge test contents in terms of the demands they place on the pupils for whom the test items are intended.

Anyone who conducts a similar analysis, will find it useful to accumulate a collection of examples which illustrate 'case law' – that is to say, items whose categorization is difficult. Case law can then be invoked when items from other tests are considered, so that a common conceptual framework is used across all the tests reviewed. Domain might be classified in the following terms.

Number – counting and ordering; operations on integers, fractions, decimals and percentages; choice of operation; estimation and approximation; series; number bases.
Measurement – reading and interpreting scales and tabular information; using instruments; knowledge of units; knowledge of size of units with respect to one's own experience; telling the time; using a calendar.
Space – naming and recognizing plane and solid figures, and knowing their properties; calculating perimeters, areas and volumes; using scales, co-ordinates and bearings; and the use of geometry.
Algebra – using symbols; substituting in formulae; the idea of a variable; manipulation and solution of equations; obtaining a

formula or equation from a description in words; choosing and
defining symbols; drawing graphs from formulae.

Logic – satisfying multiple constraints; word problems; use of
sets; games and puzzles; reasoning; diagrammatic representations of logic.

Statistics – the calculation of averages; drawing inferences from
data; representation of statistics.

Process might classify items in the following terms.

Recall – remembering specific facts, definitions, concepts and
formulae. For example, recall is involved in questions on place
value, or the calculation of areas and volumes where little
numerical technique is required.

Technique – the use of skills such as measuring, reading tables,
geometric constructions, factorization, use of the four operations,
calculation involving whole numbers, fractions, decimals and
percentages, where the task to be performed is quite explicit, but
requires the direct application of some skill which pupils could be
reasonably expected to have acquired by the age of testing.

Comprehension – the conversion of material presented in one
form or another; the separation of relevant from irrelevant
information on an item, for the purpose of solving problems;
seeing implications of information presented. Comprehension is
involved in problems such as: choice of operation; word problems; reasoning problems; combining information; completing
series; interpreting information; and explanation.

Items can be described as *abstract* when material is presented
only in symbolic form, such as numbers or letters. (Therefore,
diagrams are never 'abstract'.) Items can be classified as *concrete*
when questions are set in some context, expected to be familiar to
the child, such as problems which involve money, time, or everyday
objects.

Tests can often be rejected for school use because they fail to
satisfy users' requirements about coverage of domains or processes
(or for faults such as datedness of content, and technical inad-
equacy). Tests which appear to be suitable should be inspected
before widespread use. No test can include all the subskills which
every teacher wishes to assess; it is important, however, that tests
assess abilities which one deems to be important, and do not focus
unduly on aspects of mathematical attainment which are not valued
highly.

The process of test standardization

Standardization refers to the process of establishing a baseline of performance on the test, against which pupil performance can be judged. It is a difficult and time-consuming process, and is rarely done well.

Consider a test which is being developed to assess the arithmetic skills of 10-year-olds in the United Kingdom. Which factors would be expected to affect the score of different groups of children on this test? An obvious factor is the curriculum which children have followed – schools which place heavy emphasis on arithmetic, and which test arithmetic skills on a regular basis either in class or via regular homework are likely to produce children who perform better on such measurements than children who devote little time to the mastery of arithmetic. The general ability of the children taking the test will also be reflected in test scores; so one might reasonably expect that children who are good at a wide range of things will also be good at arithmetic. Both of these factors will be reflected in the attainment of different schools. One might expect differences in overall attainment between different LEAs and, within the same LEA, schools with markedly different catchment areas (e.g. inner city versus rural versus urban).

The test constructor is faced with the task of obtaining a large, representative sample of pupils on which to standardize tests. If the test is intended for use with all 10-year-olds in the United Kingdom then a large, random sample of pupils' test results should be taken. Testing large samples of pupils is extremely time-consuming, as well as expensive. A number of devices are employed to reduce the time taken to obtain the standardization data and to reduce the constructor's costs. One such device is to look at the composition of the target population, then to select a sample for standardization purposes which matches this composition. For example, if data are available nationally on the number of schools with different sorts of catchment areas, then the test constructor can set out to make sure that this composition is reflected in the sample used. Issues such as the nature of the school curriculum, of course, are far harder to take into account; the best defence which the test constructor has is to ensure that the sample is taken from a large number of different schools. From the test constructor's viewpoint this poses considerable problems; as more schools and LEAs become involved, the administrative load increases and more development time is needed.

It is clear from reading a number of test manuals that many test authors resolve their difficulties by confining their standardization sample quite considerably – for example to a single LEA or to a particular town – worse still, from the user's viewpoint, manuals are often quite vague about the nature of the standardizing sample; and about the sampling design (e.g. whether a random or a stratified sample was used). Few test authors comment on the extent to which they believe their sample to be representative of the larger population to which they wish to generalize their results.

These comments are of direct relevance to norm-referenced tests, but are less relevant to diagnostic tests, although even here some indication of the incidence of different kinds of misconception should be supplied – hopefully based on representative samples rather than unrepresentative ones. In general it is the case that tests are standardized on non-random samples which are not necessarily representative of the population for which the test is intended. When choosing a test for use in school, the description of the standardizing sample and the process of standardization should be a prime consideration. A serious problem with test manuals is that they often omit important information to allow the user to judge the representativeness of the standardization sample.

UNDERSTANDING TEST SCORES

Suppose that a test constructor has obtained test scores from a large, representative sample of 10-year-olds. Table 2.1 shows how these data might look. Each entry in the table shows the number of pupils whose scores fell within a particular score band.

No individual score has much meaning on its own. A score of 0 on any test cannot be interpreted to mean complete absence of ability. Nor can one conclude that a score of 80 is necessarily twice as good as a score of 40. Similarly, the difference between scores of 80 and 70 may not have the same significance as the difference between scores of 70 and 60. It is clear that a score of 60 does not mean 60 per cent of some perfection known only to the tester. Nor does it mean that some pupil has mastered 60 per cent of the total curriculum perfectly. Suppose Jo scores 60 on literacy and 80 on numeracy. We can draw no conclusions at all about relative strengths in literacy and numeracy or about relative performance in each compared to peers. Most children have had the experience of trying to explain to parents that say, although they came third in literacy they got 60 – yet a score of 80 in numeracy only put them in 18th position in the

Table 2.1:   Raw scores from a sample of 1000 pupils aged 10.0 years

Range of raw scores	Number of pupils
78 and over	40
70–77	70
62–69	120
54–61	170
46–53	200
38–45	170
30–37	120
22–29	70
21 and below	40

same class. The process of standardization sets out to resolve some of these problems by simplifying the data to facilitate interpretation and use. One simplification is to estimate 'test age'. Each group of children in a given age range will produce a spread of scores. It is easy to calculate the mean (or median) score for each age range, which is a reflection of the attainment of 'typical' group members. On average, older children have higher scores than younger ones. (Test items which are not easier for older children are usually weeded out of the test at an early stage. Such items – for example on statistics or fractions – are thought provoking!)

This process can be repeated for each age group, and summarized in table form.

Table 2.2:   Average scores achieved at different ages

Age	9:06	9:09	10:00	10:03	10:06	10:09	11:00	11:03	11:06
Average score	44	47	50	53	56	59	62	65	68

Suppose we now give the same test to someone who obtains a score of 65. We can look this score up under Average Score in Table 2.2, and read off the age at which pupils of average ability obtain such a score; this is then the test age of the pupil. Of course, a pupil can have a test age that is higher (or lower) than their chronological age. The direction of the difference (older than test age; younger than test age) tells the tester whether the pupil is ahead or behind his or her peers; the size of the difference gives some indication of the extent of the discrepancy. So what is wrong with this procedure?

First, the term 'test age' (or 'mental age' or similar) can be misleading. It would be wrong to assume that a bright eight-year-old were functioning in the same way as, say, a twelve-year-old of average ability, or that a retarded adult were functioning in the same way as an average four-year-old. Secondly, the average score of each age group need not be representative of the group as a whole – the score distribution may be skewed, for example. The test age also fails to capture any information about the range of test scores obtained either from pupils of the same age as the person being tested or from the pupils of their supposed test age.

Comparison with peers is one of the commonest reasons for testing. This gives rise to one of the commonest forms of reporting scores – the use of the Normal distribution to standardize raw scores into a form which is readily understood. The Normal distribution is shown in Figure 2.1. Two features of this distribution are particularly important: the mean, which is the arithmetic average; and the standard deviation, which is a measure of the spread of scores.

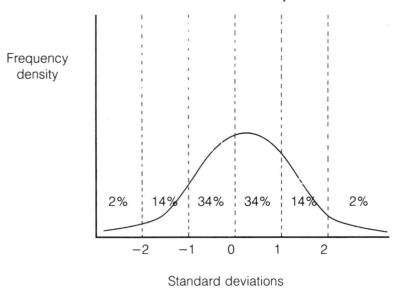

Standard deviations

Figure 2.1:   The Normal distribution

Percentages refer to the proportion of the population whose scores fall within each division.

Scores obtained on tests often approximate a Normal distribution; test authors usually choose items in order to produce Normal score distributions on their tests. This distribution is used because it has a number of useful statistical properties. For example, if scores from two or more Normal distributions are combined together, a third Normal distribution is obtained, whose mean and standard deviation can be calculated in advance; and the Normal distribution allows easy comparison of raw scores on different tests which are quite different in their means and degree of spread.

It is relatively easy to calculate the mean and standard deviation for any collection of scores. If the shape of the score distribution is approximately Normal then the percentage of scores which are greater (or less) than a given score can be determined in a straightforward way.

Figure 2.1 shows the percentage of scores which fall between different boundaries marked by standard deviations on the figure. Any raw score can be converted to a score in terms of standard deviations simply by subtracting from it the raw score mean, then by dividing by the standard deviation. Such scores are referred to as deviation scores or as standardized (or standard) scores. Test scores which have a mean of zero and which extend from -3 to $+3$ are not very easy to work with, nor are they satisfactory to deal with psychologically. Imagine working hard on a test and feeling that you have made good progress only to discover your score is -0.33! So it is common practice to adjust scores so that they have a mean of 100 and a standard deviation of 15. This practice has no effect on the shape of the distribution, and hence makes no difference to the percentage of scores which fall between different boundaries, as long as we talk in terms of standard deviations. For example, if a test has a mean of 100 and a standard deviation of 15, the highest scoring two per cent of pupils will have scores over 130 (i.e. two standard deviations above the mean: $2 \times 15 + 100$). If the mean were 100 and the standard deviation were 25, then the most able two per cent would have scores over 150 ($2 \times 25 + 100$).

This practice allows the test constructor to present test scores in a way which is readily interpretable to users. Armed with a table of cumulative percentages for deviation scores on the Normal distribution (called test norms) the user can readily interpret the score of any pupil in terms of the test scores obtained by his or her peers. It is common, therefore, for test manuals to present tables which relate raw test scores to a Normal score distribution; by convention, these are standardized to have a mean of 100 and a standard deviation of 15.

The relative achievements of pupils of different ages can then be compared by comparing each child to his or her own peers. So in Table 2.3 we can see that a child aged 9:07 with a raw score of 35 has a standardized or 'standard' score of 105, whereas a child of age 10:10 with the same raw score has a test score of 100. This is easy to interpret by saying that the former pupil has achieved a score which is likely to be bettered by about 46 per cent of children of the same age, whereas the latter has achieved a score which is likely to be bettered by 50 per cent of the children of his or her own age.

Scores in a form referring to the percentage of pupil scores which fall below the score of a particular pupil are referred to as percentile scores (or centiles, or percentiles or percentile ranks). A percentile score is simply a rank order expressed in percentage terms. For example, a pupil with a standard score of 130 will have a percentile score of about 98; the pupil who is exactly in the middle of the group (i.e. at the median) will have a percentile score of 50.

Percentile scores have the following advantages: they are easy to understand (which makes them easy to explain to people who have little statistical knowledge); they are easy to compute if the score distribution is Normal; they can be interpreted accurately irrespective of the shape of the distribution of scores. They have the following disadvantages: they magnify differences near the mean which may be quite unimportant; they reduce the apparent size of large differences in the tails of the distribution which might be of great significance; percentile scores are also less easy to use for the purposes of statistical analysis.

Standard scores have the following advantages: differences in standard score are proportional to differences in raw score; using standard scores in the calculation of averages and correlation coefficients produces the same results as those that would be obtained from the use of raw scores. They have the following disadvantages: they are hard to interpret when score distributions are skewed (another reason for test developers to adjust the score distribution until it fits the Normal distribution); some knowledge of statistics is required to interpret and understand them (although two scores expressed in terms of standard scores are easy to discuss with parents, for example).

PROFILES Some tests report pupil attainment as a simple score. Others provide subscores (sometimes called scales, or subscales) which relate to different aspects of performance. A collection of such subscores, or of scores from a number of different tests can be called a profile because the collection of scores reflects a pupil's strengths and weaknesses relative to other pupils. The availability of test norms makes it possible to compare attainment in different domains or different subjects, in comparison with one's peers. Interpreting profiles must be done with great caution, however. It is logically impossible to compare tests which measure different kinds of knowledge in terms of their absolute difficulties. All that can be done is to compare relative standings. For example, suppose that in advanced mathematics classes all the pupils were assessed in terms of their mathematical attainment and in terms of their abilities to paint a landscape; it is quite conceivable that several pupils would have far higher percentile scores on the landscape drawing test than on the mathematical attainment test. Nevertheless, it would be folly to conclude that they were better at art than at mathematics.

NORMS   When one is concerned with either absolute levels of performance, or the relative performance of members within a group such as a class, test norms must not be over valued. They must not be judged as criteria, for example. It is wrong to expect each 11-year-old to reach the average score recorded for 11-year-olds – obviously 50 per cent of the pupils in the standardizing sample fell below this score. Similarly, average class performance which is at or above some reported average need not necessarily be grounds for self-congratulation since norms are most unlikely to reflect the best attainments that could be made with the most effective teaching.

USING INFORMATION ABOUT STANDARDIZATION

A test manual should be quite explicit about the samples on which the test was standardized. Information should include details of age differences, sex, and level of expertise. However, even when test constructors have gone to the trouble to obtain truly representative samples which control for variation in educational attainment, regional variations and socio-economic considerations, the user cannot necessarily assume such data to be representative of their own pupils. The user must judge whether the standardization group is made up of members with whom the current testees can reasonably be compared, whether the sample chosen represents an appropriate population, and whether the sample is large enough.

It is clear that pupils' ages will be related to their attainment; in general pupils' attainment increases as they get older. However, the relationship between their age and their attainment is not necessarily straightforward. Two factors obviously affect this relationship;

Table 2.3:   Raw score–standard score conversion table

Age Range 9:07–10:10

RAW SCORE	AGE IN YEARS AND COMPLETED MONTHS AT THE DATE OF THE TEST																RAW SCORE
	9:07	9:08	9:09	9:10	9:11	10:00	10:01	10:02	10:03	10:04	10:05	10:06	10:07	10:08	10:09	10:10	
0																	0
1																	1
2																	2
3																	3
4	70	70															4
5	72	72	71	71	71	70	70	70									5
6	74	74	73	73	72	72	72	71	71	71	70	70	70				6
7	75	75	75	74	74	74	73	73	73	72	72	72	71	71	71	70	7
8	77	77	76	76	76	75	75	74	74	74	73	73	73	72	72	72	8
9	78	78	78	77	77	77	76	76	76	75	75	74	74	74	73	73	9
10	80	79	79	79	78	78	78	77	77	76	76	76	75	75	75	74	10
11	81	81	80	80	79	79	79	78	78	78	77	77	77	76	76	76	11
12	82	82	81	81	81	80	80	80	79	79	79	78	78	77	77	77	12
13	83	83	82	82	82	81	81	81	80	80	80	79	79	79	78	78	13
14	84	84	84	83	83	82	82	82	81	81	81	80	80	80	79	79	14
15	85	85	85	84	84	83	83	83	82	82	82	81	81	81	80	80	15
16	86	86	86	85	85	85	84	84	83	83	83	82	82	82	81	81	16
17	87	87	87	86	86	85	85	85	84	84	84	83	83	83	82	82	17
18	88	88	88	87	87	86	86	86	85	85	85	84	84	84	83	83	18
19	89	89	88	88	88	87	87	87	86	86	86	85	85	85	84	84	19
20	90	90	89	89	89	88	88	88	87	87	87	86	86	86	85	85	20
21	91	91	90	90	90	89	89	89	88	88	88	87	87	86	86	86	21
22	92	92	91	91	91	90	90	90	89	89	88	88	88	87	87	87	22

	10:10	10:09	10:08	10:07	10:06	10:05	10:04	10:03	10:02	10:01	10:00	9:11	9:10	9:09	9:08	9:07	
23	88	88	88	89	89	89	90	90	90	91	91	92	92	92	93	93	23
24	89	89	89	90	90	90	91	91	91	92	92	92	93	93	94	94	24
25	90	90	90	91	91	91	92	92	92	93	93	93	94	94	94	95	25
26	90	91	91	92	92	92	93	93	93	94	94	94	95	95	95	96	26
27	91	92	92	92	93	93	94	94	94	95	95	95	96	96	96	97	27
28	92	93	93	93	94	94	95	95	95	96	96	96	97	97	97	98	28
29	93	94	94	94	95	95	95	96	96	97	97	97	98	98	98	99	29
30	94	95	95	95	96	96	96	97	97	98	98	98	99	99	99	100	30
31	95	96	96	96	97	97	98	98	98	99	99	99	100	100	100	101	31
32	96	97	97	98	98	98	99	99	99	100	100	100	101	101	101	102	32
33	98	98	98	99	99	99	100	100	100	101	101	101	102	102	102	103	33
34	99	99	99	100	100	100	101	101	101	102	102	103	103	103	104	104	34
35	100	100	101	101	101	102	102	102	103	103	103	104	104	104	105	105	35
36	101	101	102	102	102	103	103	103	104	104	105	105	105	106	106	106	36
37	102	103	103	103	104	104	104	105	105	105	106	106	106	107	107	108	37
38	104	104	104	105	105	105	106	106	106	107	107	107	108	108	109	109	38
39	105	105	106	106	106	107	107	107	108	108	109	109	109	110	110	110	39
40	106	107	107	108	108	108	109	109	109	110	110	110	111	111	111	112	40
41	108	108	109	109	109	110	110	111	111	111	112	112	112	113	113	113	41
42	110	110	111	111	111	112	112	112	113	113	113	114	114	114	115	115	42
43	112	112	112	113	113	113	114	114	114	115	115	116	116	116	117	117	43
44	114	114	114	115	115	115	116	116	116	117	117	118	118	118	119	119	44
45	116	116	117	117	117	118	118	118	119	119	119	120	120	120	121	121	45
46	118	119	119	119	120	120	120	121	121	121	122	122	123	123	123	124	46
47	121	121	122	122	122	123	123	123	124	124	125	125	125	126	126	126	47
48	124	125	125	125	126	126	126	127	127	127	128	128	128	129	129	129	48
49	128	129	129	129	130	130	130	131	131	132	132	132	133	133	133	134	49
50	136	136	136	137	137	137	138	138	138	139	139	139	140	140			50

one is the time in the school year when testing takes place (either when the standardization of the test took place or when testing for particular purposes is to take place); the other is the age of a pupil with respect to his or her classmates. Most teachers will be familiar with the effects of the school year on pupil attainment: it has often been remarked that the six-week summer break restores pupil interest in, and motivation for, academic matters; it also seems to have a remarkable cleansing effect on the memory! As well as factors imposed on pupils' rates of learning such as times of the year when they receive direct instruction, there are appreciable differences in rates of attainment within individuals over time. Progress is not necessarily linear; it is quite commonly characterized by spurts and plateaux. A further complication is introduced by each child's position in the class with respect to his or her peers. Also, think about the problems of transfer between primary and secondary school. The attainments of younger children at secondary school and older children at primary school, where these age ranges overlap (as is often the case when comparisons are made across LEAs which have different school systems) show that type of school, too, affects test performance.

A purist would recommend that a test user should administer the test at the same time of the school year as the standardization sample was tested, for the norms to be useful. (The same purist will be surprised at how few test manuals provide this information.) Test manuals should give separate norms for different types of school – primary or secondary, for example – where such data might be relevant, or at least an assurance that the possibility of different standardizations for both groups have been examined and found to be unnecessary. Many test authors adopt the method of standardizing test scores which assumes a linear relationship between the test score and pupil age – thus ignoring the likelihood of seasonal effects and of different school experiences.

Test users are strongly recommended only to use tests which have been standardized on a sample of direct interest. Little credibility should be given to test norms which have been extrapolated, rather than directly derived.

Even when all relevant data are provided and are judged to be satisfactory, some problems remain concerning their use. It is clear that the notion of norms involves not just questions of simple statistical technique, but also conceptual issues. Suppose one were teaching in an inner city school with a large immigrant population, and that many of the children in one's class had English as a poor second language. How useful are norms based on similar populations? Is it enough to know that one's class is performing on a par with classes of a similar composition in other inner city areas, or is information about the total population more relevant? The interpretation that is made of test scores depends very much on one's purpose for testing in the first place. Suppose one finds that girls achieve significantly lower scores than boys in geometry tests. It is adequate to use tables of norms developed on girls and boys separately, or is the difference between the two inherently interesting, and a cause for concern?

Reliability and validity

RELIABILITY

Test scores are measures of attainment, and like all other forms of measurement, are associated with a certain degree of inaccuracy. If one measures the length of a table in terms of the number of hand spans which it takes, then multiplies by an appropriate number which corresponds to the hand span (e.g. eight inches) a reasonable estimate of the length of the table can be produced, but one that is likely to inspire less confidence than a measurement of the same table made using a steel ruler. Similarly, if one is measuring the size of small objects, a steel ruler will provide a crude measure compared with that obtainable using a micrometer. Of course, it is rather hard measuring tables using a micrometer! So different measuring devices are constructed for different purposes, and have different degrees of accuracy inherent in them. This observation is particularly relevant to tests concerned with the assessment of attainment. Far too often a test constructor will present the test user with an estimate of a pupil's level of attainment without offering any indication of the accuracy level of this measurement. Individual test scores should always be given between two boundaries, rather than having an exact value. To return to the example of measuring the table: if one is measuring the table in terms of hand spans, it can be asserted that the table length is 56 +/−4 inches with a great deal of confidence; for the steel rule one might report 57 +/− ¼ inch, with the same degree of confidence. It is clear that different degrees of accuracy are necessary for different purposes. If one needs to know whether the table will fit on to a furniture van then the information provided by hand span measures is likely to be sufficient; if veneer is to be cut to fit the table top then the level of accuracy obtainable from a steel rule is probably necessary.

How can the reliability of a test be assessed? This straightforward question has no simple answer. Reliability is intimately concerned with the purposes of testing and test validity; shortly it will be argued that each test has many reliabilities. Practical guidance can be offered to avoid over-emphasis on exact test scores, however.

Suppose a large number of people are asked to measure the table using our steel rule; one can then plot their answers, and will probably produce a normal distribution similar to the one drawn in Figure 2.1. Notice that the original rationale for drawing Figure 2.1 was to illustrate the spread of ability across individuals – here, the same individual (the table) is being assessed, but one still gets a spread of measures. This spread of measures – called the error variance (for obvious reasons), should be smaller than the variance in individual scores. The standard deviation of these different measures is called the standard error of measurement (SEM). The larger the SEM, the lower the accuracy of measurement, and the less confidence one can have about the result of any particular test score.

It is not necessary to administer the same measure (test) repeatedly to the same individual in order to estimate the SEM of the test (this procedure would probably produce invalid results anyway, for psychological reasons such as boredom or fatigue or perhaps learning and memory factors). It can be calculated directly from the reliability coefficient, which can be obtained in much easier ways. When scores are available from people who are assessed on two separate occasions, an estimate of the reliability of the test can be obtained. For example, if wildly different rank orders were obtained there would be suspicion that the test is an inaccurate measure or that the behaviour tested is unstable over time; if the rank orders remain the same, one can have more confidence in the test. So one approach to estimating the reliability of a test is to administer it to a large group of pupils on different occasions, or to administer equivalent ('parallel') forms of the test. The extent to which the two forms of scores agree is an index of measurement accuracy which we can use to estimate the SEM. Of course, the way in which data are collected to assess reliability is important.

If two forms of test are given on the same day there may well be carry-over effects from one test to the next – pupils may remember items and the way they anwered them either correctly or incorrectly. There may also be effects of general fatigue.

If tests are given one year apart there may well be changes in the underlying abilities of the children who are assessed.

There are a number of other methods for assessing the reliability of a test which differ in the psychological or statistical assumptions they make.

If it is assumed that every item in a test is no more and no less important than every other item, and that items are 'locally independent', i.e. that the ability to succeed on one test item does not depend on its position with respect to other test items (as a counter example, for many pupils, the test item 91 × 11 would be considerably easier if it were preceded by the item 90 × 11 than if it were preceded by the item 19 × 11) then reliability of certain kinds of tests can be estimated by measure of internal consistency. These measures compare performance on different items within a test. A variety of formulae are available to allow internal reliability to be quantified, for example Kuder–Richardson formulae 20 and 21 (KR-20, KR-21).

One can distinguish conceptually between *speed tests* and *power tests* (although most tests assess components of both speed and power). In a *speed test* the time allocated for the test is limited and pupils are required to complete as many items as they can within a limited amount of time. In principle, given sufficient time, each pupil would be expected to complete every item successfully. In contrast, a *power test* is one in which test items vary considerably in difficulty, and in which items are presented in an approximate order of difficulty. It is to be expected that different individuals will make little or no progress beyond certain test items, even if given unlimited time to work on the items.

Measures of internal consistency have been designed for use with power tests. Such measures should never be applied to speed tests, because the estimate of the reliability which is produced will be misleading and can easily, spuriously suggest that a speed test is perfectly reliable. Some test manuals quote KR-20 and KR-21 coefficients to indicate the reliability of speed tests, however, these cannot be interpreted sensibly.

High internal consistency shows that test items are assessing similar skills and processes. This is not always a desirable attribute of tests in education, since this high internal consistency is bought at the cost of a narrowing of content and process. There seems to be little point in measuring a tiny aspect of attainment with high reliability (unless perhaps the focus is diagnosis).

Other measures of reliability involve repeated administration of either the same test or parallel forms of test. Here, too, there are problems. First there is the problem of ensuring that tests are adequately parallel. A second problem is associated with students remembering the way they solved problems on earlier tests. The third is associated with genuine changes in attainment which might well have occurred between administrations of the test.

Each of these different measures shows that tests do not have a single reliability, and illustrate the problems of assessing measurement error.

It is quite easy to obtain very high estimates of test reliabilities which are false. For example, if a sample of pupils with a very wide range of attainment is tested on two separate occasions, then the scores obtained by individuals on the first and second occasion are likely to be strongly related to each other. Using an estimate derived from this sort of procedure as an appropriate estimate for, say, a class test in a school which streams its pupils on the basis of mathematical attainment, would lead to serious errors. Overestimates of reliability can also be obtained unwittingly by using a wide age range (which is the same problem under a different guise). Test manuals, therefore, should be explicit in their description of the way in which reliability coefficients are obtained, and test users should ensure that the claims made concerning reliability are sensible, and apply to their particular circumstances.

It is important that an estimate of the likely accuracy of measurement be incorporated into any report of the test score. It would be displeasing to find that a bookcase, reported to be 47 inches wide, bought to fit into an alcove 48 inches wide, was actually 49 inches wide because the vendor measured it by handspan, not ruler. A report of 47 inches +/− 4 inches would have avoided the upset. Since pupils are far more important than bookcases, any decisions about allocation to different educational experiences which are based on some assessment procedure, should take account of the SEM of these procedures.

Test manuals should always include information about the SEM, and the way it was calculated. Even when this information is provided, caution is required in its application. The reason for caution is that the error of measurement is different at different parts of the score distribution. This perhaps sounds paradoxical, but some reflection will show why this is the case. Most tests are designed to discriminate amongst pupils in the middle of the attainment range, and so most test items are selected with this purpose in mind. Discrimination amongst the highest and amongst the lowest attaining pupils, therefore, is left to rather few test items. Discovering test items which discriminate amongst pupils at the extremes of the score distribution is usually a secondary task for test designers (and requires the testing of large numbers of exceptional pupils) and so the few discriminating items are often less valid than items chosen to distinguish amongst pupils in the middle range. It follows from this that extreme scores should be treated with more caution than intermediate scores. Any score which is more than two standard deviations above the mean should not be over-interpreted. The test user should not believe necessarily that a pupil with a score of 150 has an appreciably higher attainment than the pupil with a score of 140. In the middle of the range, however, the user can be confident that a pupil with a score of 110 has performed appreciably better than one with a score of 100. This observation about the reliability of the scores in different parts of the range is relevant to tests which are aimed to assess attainment over a wide range of pupil skill. Of course, when tests have been developed to discriminate between high (or low) attaining pupils, test designers will have taken some pains to ensure that large samples of pupils of relevant ability have been used in the standardization process. Earlier comments about the reliability of different parts of the distribution will still apply to the extremes (notably the end of the distribution away from the mean) of this new sample. So tests can be used to discriminate between high attaining pupils, if they are designed to do so; tests which are designed for assessing the attainment of a normal range of pupils are less well suited for discriminating amongst the most (and the least) able pupils.

VALIDITY

The validity of a test is taken to mean the extent to which the test measures what it is supposed to measure. Before anyone can judge the validity of a test they must set out to decide what purposes the test is to serve. The notion of validity has no meaning outside the purposes of the tester. Whosoever uses tests regularly should engage in the salutary activity of trying to articulate the processes which underlie performance of the test items. Even if one doesn't get as far as testing these hypotheses – for example, by constructing tests which sample these sub-skills more directly – this reflective process is likely to stimulate thinking more clearly about the purposes for testing, and indeed about one's implicit theories of education.

The four broad classes of validation which are commonly referred to are surface validity, content validity, predictive validity, and construct validity. *Surface validity* is what a test appears to measure; this might be quite unrelated to other forms of validity! *Content validity* refers to the particular items themselves, and is particularly important in education. For example, it would be hard to justify an end-of-term test which failed to sample content or process from the syllabus for that term. *Predictive validity* refers to the ability of a test to predict some future outcome – for example, scholastic attainment, the probability of completing a particular training course, or some measure of on-the-job performance. *Construct validation* requires the test scores to be integrated into a particular theoretical framework. It follows that the construct validity of tests can change as constructs about the nature of mathematical attainment change.

SURFACE VALIDITY If people taking tests feel they are unfair, or are sampling behaviours which are irrelevant, then the validity of the test is likely to be lower than if they feel that they are being fairly tested.

If test items are seen to be interesting then test taking is likely to be far more pleasant than if the items are inherently dull. Test constructors must persuade everybody concerned with the test – pupils, parents, teachers, further education tutors, employers, and often goverments – that what is being measured is a fair and sensible thing to be measured and that processes – broadly defined – of the assessment scheme are fair to all concerned.

CONTENT VALIDITY Test developers have a responsibility to define their domain of interest clearly and to describe this domain to the users as follows:

- instructions to the test taker;
- the nature of the tasks, stimuli, and the testing situation;
- the nature of the responses to be made;
- the scoring procedures.

When attempting to assess some rather general skills, such as skills in mathematics, it is probably necessary for the test author to describe some sub-divisions of interest if a representative test is to be produced. Next, items from each of these sub-divisions have to be selected. As the range of the domain increases, the test constructor has more problems in sampling items in a representative fashion. For example, suppose one were interested in testing mathematical reasoning; the range of content areas where one might test this is quite wide, as is the nature of the test items which one might construct. In such cases when one examines the content validity of a test it can be hard to judge whether the test constructor has adequately sampled the domain of interest. Subsidiary questions might be as follows: Does the test over-emphasize any sub-division of the domain? Are there any aspects of the test which are irrelevant to the domain of interest? For example, in a reasoning test the use of technical vocabulary in problems may increase item difficulty in a way which is irrelevant to the logical demands of the item.

These issues are also relevant to the design of examination papers. The Examination Boards' provision of a syllabus and past papers is intended to show teachers in schools the range of skills to be acquired. The skills which must be exhibited to perform well on the test are implicit in the nature of the questions which are posed; skills which never appear in the examinations are implicitly not valued.

Item formats are also important. Presenting items in the form of pictures or words, or other kinds of representation can have dramatic effects on the item difficulty; it can also have an effect on the nature of the skills assessed. The amount of time allowed for a test also reflects the skills assessed. Suppose pupils are presented with a page of sums and are allowed just a short time to complete them. Students may well gain marks via fast though inaccurate performance compared to students who work through each item carefully ensuring that their responses are correct. The educational value of repeated uses of such tests might well be extremely limited (or indeed, negative).

PREDICTIVE VALIDITY The most obvious role for tests as predictive devices focuses on their use in vocational guidance, the selection of employees, in educational tests for entry to further education, and for diagnostic use. (Diagnosis of particular skill impairments or systematic misconceptions has little use unless it is associated with remediation.) The process of establishing the predictive validity of tests is straightforward. Test scores are simply correlated with external criteria. It is clear that any judgements based on validation against external criteria should begin by challenging each criterion in turn. How is it derived? How stable is it? Is this the only external criterion available? Is there a cluster of criteria which could be used? One should also ask if high predictive validity implies that the test is inherently valuable, or if it suggests that there is something wrong with the course of study, or the way the job is performed. Suppose that a test on fractions is shown to be highly predictive of people who perform well on a course for lathe operators. Our first questions are likely to be about the design of the training course – we should ask whether unreasonable computational demands are being placed on trainees who are attempting to acquire manual skills, and whether the course can be redesigned to reduce the demands being made (e.g., by the provision of calculators). In short, high predictive validity may well lead to a redesign which in turn leads to a reduction in predictive validity. This apparent paradox results from the earlier requirement that the purpose of all validation studies is to understand tests better – not simply to justify their existence. (In today's bracing economic climate, it would be disingenuous not to refer to the role of tests in rejecting candidates on some quasi-rational basis; discussions of predictive validity are a secondary consideration for this use of tests.)

As well as long-term studies of predictive validity, it is common to carry out concurrent studies. As before there are a number of forms of concurrent validity. One form is to examine the performance on the test of acknowledged 'experts' and 'novices'. A second form is to compare performance on the test in question with performance on tests which purport to measure similar attributes. This latter procedure is somewhat dubious – if most tests have their validity established via comparison with tests given similar labels by their test constructors, this provides little outside evidence that what they are measuring is what they claim to measure. This procedure only shows that they all seem to measure the same thing. Demonstrating the existence of strong predictive relationships should not be seen as an end in itself. It is necessary to inquire why such relationships apply.

CONSTRUCT VALIDITY This refers to the relationship of the test to a whole network of ideas about what it measures. Robust theories are ones which offer schemes of measurement for theoretical constructs ('force', 'velocity', 'mass') as well as testable statements about the interrelationships between these variables ('acceleration is proportional to the force applied'). The same is true for theories of behaviour. For example, suppose one believes that 'introverts' are best at working on their own on familiar problems, and that 'extroverts' perform best in group work on unfamiliar problems. Both 'introversion' and 'extroversion' are constructs. If a test exists which purports to measure these constructs, and evidence is also gathered on the performance of individuals on both familiar tasks and unfamiliar tasks, performed either alone or in groups, evidence can be collected to confirm or negate the predictions made. Confirmation supports both the theory itself, and the claim that the test is the measure of the constructs of introversion and extroversion. This process is referred to as construct validation.

Construct validation is rarely discussed by test authors, despite its centrality to the whole purpose of assessment. Consider the challenge posed by reliable score differences between boys and girls. What should one do about such differences when designing a test? One strategy is to reject all items which favour one sex or the other. This is not necessarily a good thing to do. If the construct validity of the test has been established on rational grounds, then rejecting test items simply because they discriminate between males and females seems to be a rather irrational practice. A far better practice would be to explore the nature of these differences and perhaps look for the mechanisms which underlie them. For example, a number of studies show the superiority of males over females in a variety of tasks which require the use of spatial skills, such as items requiring mental rotations, paper folding, sketching an object from different perspectives and the like; tests which involve verbal comprehension often favour females. Discarding all tests which involve spatial skills from tests of mathematics would seem to be a rather thoughtless practice, as would the removal of all items which relate to verbal comprehension from tests of English, simply because girls often perform better on such tasks.

ARE RELIABILITY AND VALIDITY REALLY DISTINCT?

A variety of forms of reliability and of validity have just been described as if they were separate; however this is far from the case. Since the essence of validation is to understand and explain what is measured, and to relate this to some more general theory of the instructional process and the nature of individual differences, some estimate of the reliability of measures is an inherent aspect of any discussion of validity. It is obvious, therefore, that all these strands of validity and reliability are intimately intertwined, and have no real separate identity, despite their traditional divorce in test manuals and in literature on tests and testing in general.

From the viewpoint of test evaluation, it is necessary to read those sections of the test manual which relate to the purposes for which the test was constructed, to reliability, and to validity. Few manuals discuss validity adequately and judgements are left to the reader. Decisions to use a particular test should be based on one's purposes and on judgements about validity and reliability.

Using tests

ADMINISTRATION

The assessment of someone's weight can be done reasonably reliably with rather little effort on his or her part – the person need only stand on a pair of scales. On the other hand, if one wishes to obtain an estimate of mathematical attainment, a great deal of cooperation is required. Unless the person being tested values the activity and wishes to demonstrate his or her competence, the activity is doomed from the outset.

Tests are usually designed to be administered to individuals or groups. Whilst group tests can easily be administered to individuals, tests designed for individual administration can rarely be given to groups. Most tests are presented in written form, although some are given orally, especially those intended for younger pupils, or pupils with reading difficulties.

Administering tests and examinations requires some skill; it is usually worthwhile practising test administration, and writing down the sequence of operations to be performed as a list, which can then be checked off during testing. Most test manuals either specify that the test is timed, and state the duration, or offer estimates of how long an untimed test is likely to take. (Settling the class, and reading out test instructions takes time, too, so it is important to ensure that the lesson is long enough for the whole testing session.) Most tests are designed for school use, and so can be administered within a double period. Longer tests, and tests designed for younger pupils, can often be taken in two parts, split, for example, by break-time. Manuals are usually explicit about the equipment which pupils are allowed to use, such as pencils, erasers, rulers and calculators. Care should be taken to abide by these recommendations; results are likely to be uninformative if pupils require rulers marked in millimetres and have not got them, or if calculators are used to solve items meant to assess mental arithmetic skills.

The test setting is important. Pupils must have sufficient space to work, have no problems writing, be able to read the test booklet, be able to see and hear the instructor, and be deterred from copying from others. When possible, testing should take place in a familiar room (preferably the one where mathematics is usually taught) and should be administered by a familiar teacher. Testing large groups can pose problems, because pupils may be unwilling to ask questions on issues about which they are uncertain. The pupils' state of mind is important. Pupils who are tired, or who have just engaged in high levels of physical or mental activity are likely to perform worse than pupils who are rested and alert. High levels of anxiety are also likely to contribute to test unreliability. Testing pupils within one week of arrival at a new school should always be avoided. The unfamiliarity of a school setting and the teacher are likely to produce not only lower overall results, but results which are inconsistent with results taken two weeks later when pupils have had more chance to settle in.

The importance of these factors should not be underestimated. For example, suppose one were interested in carrying out a study on the efficacy of particular forms of teaching. If initial performance were judged on the basis of a test given by an unfamiliar tester in unfamiliar circumstances for the 'experimental' condition and by a familiar teacher in a familiar setting for the 'conventional' condition, then lower estimates of attainment are likely to be obtained in the former category. Since a common practice in educational research is to look for gains in scores, this lower initial performance, produced by inappropriate initial testing, is likely to convince a naive researcher that the 'experimental' condition has had a significant effect – by bringing a low achieving group up to the level of a higher achieving group in a relatively short period of time.

Describing the purpose of the test to pupils is well worthwhile. This is particularly so if the test is being used for some diagnostic purpose rather than simply to put pupils in rank order with respect to each other. Pupils who can see that tests are intended to further learning in a direct way are likely to respond positively.

It can help to explain the nature of standardized tests and to point out, before one embarks on the formal aspect of the test, that you are going to adopt a role of 'the fair tester' and to say that, for the test to be fair to everyone who takes it, everyone must receive exactly the same instructions. From this friendly (and honest) beginning one can then switch into 'tester mode'. Of course, the 'tester mode' should not be presented in an authoritarian fashion – it is important to maintain the relationship of supporting the pupils to the full without infringing the directions.

The overriding aim of standardized test instructions is to present a test in the same way to all candidates who take the test, in an atmosphere where candidates are relaxed but eager to show their skills off to the best of their abilities. Test instructions should always be given one at a time in a clear, simple format. A theatrical slowness is to be preferred to a gallop through the administration procedure. For example, 'In front of you, you will see a test booklet' (pause, hold up the booklet, count to five silently, put the booklet down on the desk), 'Check that you have an answer sheet' (hold an answer sheet up in the air, count silently to five), scan the room to ensure that everyone has an answer sheet in front of them, and so on.

Most test directions allow pupils to ask questions. In general, the best course of action is to repeat the part of the instructions which are relevant to the question. Ideally, test directions should be free from any ambiguities (unless handling ambiguity is of central interest to the test constructor). However, test directions may well be silent on important concerns to the pupils. For example: are pupils well advised to guess at items for which they cannot work out answers, or should they skip them and proceed? If the test instructions are ambiguous then the tester should refer this ambiguity back to the pupils, either by re-reading the relevant part of the administrator's script, or by instructing pupils to decide for themselves. If a decision is taken to offer specific advice based on knowledge of the way the test is scored, for example, then the tester has changed the nature of the test by adopting a non-standard procedure. If candidates are told, as a result of their questioning, that, say, there are no penalties for guessing, then a guessing strategy is likely to result in enhanced scores. Conversely, if pupils are advised to guess, and the scoring system penalises guessing heavily, then the scores may be distorted in the opposite direction by pupils adopting a particular strategy which they would not otherwise have done.

If test scores are to be related to norms provided on the test, it is important that the test be given in the way described in the test manual. However, the situation may arise that pupils being tested are failing to display skills which they have, because of factors such as the inability to understand the instructions they are given, or perhaps an unfamiliar phrasing of questions. Under such circumstances the tester would be well advised to change the format of the test administration, but to take great care to note that the test has been given in a non-standard way. If a test is given in a non-standard way, then reliance on test norms becomes an extremely risky procedure. This, however, is to be preferred to test scores obtained from pupils who were not clear about what was required of them.

SCORING

The first thing to do when considering scoring is to do the test oneself, slowly. This activity gives a better feeling for the test contents than can be obtained simply by reading through the items. Check answers against those provided in the test manual; sometimes, though rarely, the answers supplied are wrong. Next, examine the items and look for alternative 'correct' answers which pupils might reasonably make, and note any plausible alternatives. (Again, test authors have usually taken great care to avoid including such items). Finally, a few pupils who are similar in ability to, but not members of, the target group for testing should be asked to take the test. The test should then be scored with each of them, and each should be asked to explain answers which do not correspond to those in the manual. This can highlight ambiguities in the wording of questions (more often, of course, it reveals areas where pupils have yet to master mathematical skills). Pupils usually enjoy this sort of one-to-one tutorial, especially when they feel that they are helping, rather than being assessed.

The chosen test should be found to be free of defects, and can be administered to the target group. Marking a collection of answers can be time-consuming, and speed and accuracy of marking are both helped considerably by the use of a scoring key. This is a sheet which contains all the answers to the test, laid out in such a way that when it is placed alongside the pupils' answer sheet, the pupil answers, and the corresponding correct answer, are aligned. All tests should be provided with scoring keys (rather than just a list of correct responses); some are not. In the case where a scoring key is not provided, it is well worth constructing one, even to score scripts from a single class of pupils. Test scoring systems should incorporate some scheme to avoid marker errors; for example by providing page totals for correct and wrong answers. Obtaining standard scores from the manual should also be a straightforward process.

All measurements contain errors, but usually, in the measurement of length and time, for example, one has a rough idea of how large these errors are likely to be. Test scores can vary a good deal in terms of their reliability, both across different tests and for different scores obtained on the same test, in different parts of the score distribution – scores near the mean are likely to be more reliable than those at the edge of the score distribution, for reasons described earlier. It is essential, therefore, that test scores be reported as a score interval, not just as a single score, in order to circumvent errors of interpretation when small score differences between pupils are given far greater weight than they should be. Some tests (notably those published relatively recently) build this practice into their scoring system, and label a space on the test booklet 'score band' (or similar). For tests which don't, one needs to find some estimate of the SEM in the manual, which can be used to calculate score intervals for each pupil. The following crude procedure may be followed, which improves considerably on reporting scores as integers not as score bands. Take twice the SEM from each pupil's score, to obtain the lower boundary; add twice the SEM to each pupil's score to obtain the upper boundary. This calculation produces a 95 per cent confidence interval; this can be interpreted by saying that, if the same pupil could be tested afresh on this test on twenty different occasions, the score obtained would be within the score interval just calculated on 19 of these occasions.

Evaluating tests

One can make a number of general observations about the way publishers present information about tests. Far too many tests omit information which is essential if the test user is to make informed decisions about test use. One notable gap is the lack of explanation of the designer's intentions when constructing the test. Few test manuals offer a test blueprint, or describe the process by which items were chosen; few put forward a justification for the choice of items on educational grounds. These omissions can be remedied in part, if the user is prepared to analyse test content in detail. More problematic is the omission of important technical information from test manuals, such as estimates of the SEM, and the way it was calculated. Construct validation is another important issue which is rarely considered in test manuals.

A range of other criteria on which tests can be evaluated is implicit in the earlier discussions in this chapter – for example, the clarity of the script for administration, the presence of a scoring key, advice on reporting test scores, and the uses to which test scores can be put. These concerns can be addressed via the following checklist:

- What are the purposes for which pupils are being tested? Do these agree with the purposes of the test as stated in the manual?
- Check the defined target group of the test and the age range of the standardization group. How well do they match the class to be tested?
- Look for a rationale of the content of the test items. If there isn't one, the classification system on pages 13–14 can be used to describe test content. Is the balance of items appropriate?

- Look at the sampling design – where the standardization group came from, details of sex, age, socioeconomic mix, school year. Is this a sensible basis for comparison with your class?
- Look at the instructions for administration and check that they are unambiguous.
- Look at the way the test is scored, and the way the scores are recorded (individual scores or score bands) the size of the SEM and the way it was calculated. Improve them, as necessary.
- Do the test and check the answers.

The companion volume, *A Review of Mathematics Tests* offers more detailed advice on choosing tests, as well as test reviews which describe test content, and a range of issues concerned with test development and test use. The uses for test scores are the focus of the next chapter.

3 Using Test Results

In chapter 2 (pages 9–39) a variety of styles of test were identified, including norm-referenced tests, criterion-referenced tests and diagnostic tests. Each is designed for different purposes and needs to be handled in a different manner.

Tests differ in at least two important aspects: first, in the range of items sampled (norm-referenced tests commonly sample a wide range of domains and processes; criterion-referenced and diagnostic tests usually sample narrow domains and processes); secondly, in the level of detail in the suggestions about what to do with test results (scores from norm-referenced tests are often seen to be an end in themselves; scores from criterion-referenced tests and diagnostic tests are usually associated, albeit implicitly, with plans for action). The whole point of testing is to use the results to help pupil learning; important stages in this process are to specify the nature of the abilities being assessed, (and thereby, what is being learned) and to decide what to do, given different patterns of test results.

It is impossible to offer detailed advice about ways to use every test of mathematical attainment in print. Instead, a general approach to test use will be offered, which considers the uses of norm-referenced, criterion-referenced and diagnostic tests. A theme which underlies all test use is the need to understand mathematical knowledge: how it can be described and sampled and how it is acquired and enriched and how weaknesses can be remedied. Everyone engaged in mathematical education – pupils, teachers, test designers – needs to reflect regularly up on their theories about mathematical knowledge. It follows that teachers need to discuss the learning of mathematics with pupils, as well as mathematical topics per se. Such discussions need clear foci; tests and test results can help to provide them. Assessment must not be something which is primarily of benefit to the teacher; rather it must be seen as an integral part of the whole educational enterprise. Before this becomes possible, it is necessary to develop a clear story about what it is that is being assessed.

Norm-referenced tests

Far too commonly, test authors fail to offer any description of the blueprint for test construction. Without such descriptions, the uses to which tests can be put are rather limited, because the user has little idea of what the test measures. What might one do with a set of class test scores on an ill-defined test?

Looking at class scores

The overall class results can be compared with the standardization data presented in the manual. The teacher can then discover whether the class is over- or under-performing with respect to this larger sample. (With a simple statistical test the reliability of this difference can also be assessed.) Class performance will depend on a number of factors, such as the catchment area of the school, the quality of teaching and the focus of teaching (i.e. the match between what has been taught and what is being asessed). There is little that can be done about the catchment area. Pupils in inner city areas generally perform worse than those in suburban and rural areas and changing this state of affairs is not a simple task. Would more relevant norms help? Should rural schools be compared with rural, urban with urban, and so on? Is it reasonable to ask test constructors to offer a variety of standardizations based on different communities? A problem which arises is knowing how many test norms to supply. It is common to analyse scores for girls and boys separately to see if aggregation of results is a sensible procedure; if not, separate test norms are produced. What of catchment area, etc.? As samples of pupils are analysed in more ways, (e.g. norms for West Indian born males attending rural schools) then either larger and larger numbers of pupils need to be tested, or the published test norms get less and less reliable (since they are based on smaller numbers of pupils). So the provision of more elaborate test norms would pose practical problems for test constructors. From the user's viewpoint, choice of an appropriate sample for comparison with one's own class raises awkward conceptual problems. Comparison of the performance of a whole class with a token 'national standard' should, therefore, be viewed as being a somewhat crude procedure to give a sighting of overall attainment. Little use can be made of this information as it stands: one might resolve to 'try harder', or exhort pupils to try harder if the comparison proves to be unfavourable, or one might rest on seemingly deserved laurels, if the class appears to be of above average attainment. Neither of these alternatives, on their own, is likely to be of direct benefit to pupils.

As well as comparison with test norms, one might choose to compare the performance of different classes within the school (examining the extent to which their performances differ from test norms), to get some idea about which teachers are most effective in teaching the sorts of topics being assessed. Similarly, one might choose to compare performance of schools within the same neighbourhood to assess their relative success. Both sorts of comparisons involve unresolvable problems concerning the educational goals of different teachers and the construct validity of the test used. For example, some teachers may view the test as sampling a key aspect of mathematical attainment, while others may dismiss the same test as assessing no more than mathematical technique, set out of context. In summary, it is hard to find a sensible use for class test results without a detailed analysis of test content.

Analysing tests

Some tests offer both a blueprint of the test design and a grid on each pupil's response sheet which can be used to record their relative strengths and weaknesses. Some offer a summary sheet which enables the user to review the performance of the whole class in terms of the designer's blueprint. Understanding the nature of the test is an essential prerequisite for sensible test use. Where no blueprint is available one should be constructed (even if one has been provided by the test designer, teachers may well find it useful to recategorize the items according to their own conceptual schemes). The headings used in the previous chapter offer one starting point, categorizing items by process (recall, technique and comprehension) and domain (number, measurement, space, algebra, logic, statistics). Each test item needs to be categorized according to the scheme adopted.

After this has been done, the balance of test content should be examined: are processes and domains adequately represented? No test will provide an even spread of items across each category; the purpose of this analysis is to expose excessive emphases and notable omissions in the test design. Omissions will need to be remedied by test items of one's own construction, later (or perhaps by choosing a second test with a complimentary blueprint). Before scoring a batch of tests, it is well worth constructing a table whose rows correspond to test items and whose columns relate to individual pupils. As scoring proceeds, right and wrong answers are noted on the table (a more sophisticated version would describe each wrong answer offered). When all the scripts have been scored, it is easy to calculate the difficulty of each item for this group. The most difficult items should then be analysed in terms of what makes them difficult. Perhaps the topic has not been dealt with at all in class, in this case, remedial action is obvious if one values the activity. More serious concerns are relatively poor performances in particular processes, or across domains. These will be discovered by relating performance on different test items to their place in the test blueprint. Serious weaknesses here are likely to require a revision of either the content or methods of teaching employed. Discussions with colleagues and references elsewhere in this book can offer starting points for alternative approaches to teaching.

A detailed consideration of individual items is an important aspect of any review of class progress and an analysis of what makes test items difficult is well worthwhile. By taking individual items and changing them systematically, one can explore one's own theories about difficulty and about the structure of mathematical knowledge. For example, one might explore the effects of different contexts on difficulty. Which is the harder of these two problems?

(a) find three-fifths of 30, or,

(b) Grandpa buys a bag of 30 sweets to share equally among his 5 grandchildren. Alice and Emma come in first and are given a fair share. How many sweets are left in the bag for Rosie, David and Richard?

Keeping records of class performance on different questions allows such issues to be investigated. The development of new test items, based on systematic changes to items in tests themselves (e.g. by changing the numbers in the questions, or the geometric shapes used...) allows the success of subsequent remedial teaching to be determined.

Class tests can be treated in a similar way; keeping records of questions which pupils find difficult provides a valuable resource for future use and for explorations of changes in teaching approach. Identifying items which are surprising, either in their difficulty or facility, is a useful activity. Such items can play a role for teachers which is analogous to the role played by items on diagnostic tests for pupils.

In class, a considerable amount of material is taught which pupils appear to learn and retain, at least over a short time scale. This feeling of progress contrasts markedly with surveys of mathematical attainment such as those conducted by the Assessment of Performance Unit (APU) of the Department of Education and Science (DES) and by the Concepts in Secondary Mathematics and Science Project (CSMS) carried out at Chelsea College, University of London, which both show surprisingly low levels of attainment and rather small yearly gains in pupil performance. Such surveys with their data on item difficulty make fascinating reading! Some specific wrong answers are chosen by over half of the children responding (in surveys of hundreds of children). Hart (1981) reports, 'children from very different educational backgrounds attending very different types of schools, made the same type of error and often used the same methods'.

These survey data offer a rich resource of items for classroom tests and for reflections about the nature of mathematical knowledge – stimulated, for example by considerations of what makes tasks easy or difficult. Such analyses are an essential precursor to the understanding and remediation of pupils misconceptions about mathematics.

Examining individual performance

One notable feature of tests for which standardized scores are available is that each pupil's score is based on a comparison with others in the same narrow age band (often one month) rather than with the whole age group. This can result in challenges to teacher judgements about pupil attainment, which are often made by comparison with other pupils in class. In particular, younger pupils may display considerable ability, which has gone unremarked because of a failure to consider age differences. Generally speaking though, the variance in the skills of pupils within a particular age group is usually much larger than variance of mean scores across adjacent age groups.

Discussions with each individual about their performance is best done in the context of the test blueprint. Offering a framework can help stimulate pupils' awareness of different mathematical domains and different processes. Offering pointers to topics and classes of problems which are most in need of attention from the pupil can encourage the adoption of an active role in learning and can help pupils to view their knowledge as something which *they* are responsible for. Of course, analyses of performance based on the blueprint should be treated with caution. Since very few items relate to any particular cell in the blueprint, the reliability of any pupil profile is likely to be low. Small differences should not be over-interpreted; the purpose of the analysis is to provide the basis for a discussion about gross features of pupil performance (as well as the incidental learning that one's own knowledge can, and should be studied).

Criterion-referenced tests

Criterion-referenced tests offer the promise of a direct linkage between test results and educational practice. Because the nature of what has, and has not been attained can be stated clearly, the process of communication with pupils should be facilitated. Analysis of results for the whole class show the range of competence on particular tasks. This can form the basis for future lesson plans, because the base of knowledge which everyone has attained is known, as is the spread of skills. Whole class teaching should focus on tasks at the next stage up in the task difficulty hierarchy; individual pupil work should be tailored to enrich current levels of understanding and to explore tasks at the next level.

Discussion with pupils can focus on clear task descriptions and the nature of the task hierarchy can be explained. Hopefully, this discussion will increase pupil reflection about their mathematical knowledge, as well as being the basis for a negotiation about their next learning targets.

A virtue of criterion-referenced tests is the role which they can play in communication – both with pupils and with parents – about the skills so far achieved and the skills next to be achieved. Statements about performance based on some well-defined criteria also have a role to play in smoothing pupil transitions between classes, between schools and between school and employment.

Diagnostic tests

As well as serving many of the purposes also served by criterion-referenced tests, diagnostic tests have been designed to identify particular pupil misconceptions which underlie specific errors. They are usually associated with suggestions for ways in which pupils can be confronted with errors and can be helped to overcome their associated misconceptions. The analysis of misconceptions offers a major stimulus to the growth of knowledge about mathematics for both pupils and teachers.

For illustrative purposes, problems involving multiplication and division will be considered, to reveal the scale and nature of misconceptions held by 15-year-olds. The following data are taken both from the CSMS project and from work at the Shell Centre for Mathematical Education (SCME).

- Only 29 per cent of pupils made the correct choice of multiplication to find the cost of 0.58 kg of meat at 88.2p for each kg;
- many pupils are unable to find a sensible interpretation for division by a fractional number, for example, eight divided by 0.5 is answered '4';
- faced with 'how much time does it take an athlete to run each metre if he completes an 800 metre race in 104 seconds?' most pupils chose to divide – however, they were unable to choose the correct numerator and denominator (illustrating the strategy 'always divide bigger numbers by small ones');
- 40 per cent of 15-year-olds said that three divided by 30 could not be done;
- 20 per cent said that three divided by 24 was bigger than 24 divided by three;
- about 60 per cent said that six divided by 18 and $6 \overline{\smash{\big)}\,18}$ gave the same answer;
- about 70 per cent of pupils said that multiplying 21.4 by 0.65 would make it bigger, and that dividing it by 0.65 would make it smaller;
- 15 per cent of pupils thought that 20g per penny, and 20p per gram meant that the two items were priced the same.

How might such problems be tackled? Teaching must do more than impart new knowledge; significant numbers of pupils clearly have major misconceptions in need of remediation.

An approach to testing and teaching

Consider the problems of acquiring new knowledge; two ideas are particularly important. The first is that existing knowledge and conceptual structures affect the way that new materials are perceived and learned; the second is that new experiences bring about changes in our knowledge and conceptual structures. These two processes are referred to as assimilation (analogous to the way in which the stomach digests food, whose later structure cannot be recognized as being similar to its earlier structure) and accommodation (analogous to the way that the pupil of the eye adjusts itself to different light levels). Biological analogies make it easier to understand these concepts but leave unresolved the question of when one accommodates and when one assimilates. In general, one accommodates (i.e. changes one's conceptual structures) when fresh knowledge provides strong challenges to what is in mind; so dramatic counter-examples to currently held beliefs, or coherent patterns in the world, which cannot be explained by existing beliefs, are both likely to bring about accommodation. Assimilation (interpreting new events in terms of old ideas) can be made to work when the number of counter-examples to predictions made from old beliefs are rather low. It follows, therefore, that if misconceptions are to be remedied (i.e. the mechanism of assimilation is overcome and the mechanism of accommodation stimulated) a representative sample of questions in the domain of interest is unlikely to have the desired effect because the number of cases which violate pupils' misconceptions and which therefore might cause accommodation, will be relatively small. To foster accommodation it is necessary to provide dramatic examples which violate current conceptions and to provide these examples in quantity. Examples which are most likely to be dramatic are those in which it is obvious to pupils that the results they are obtaining using particular misconceptions are at variance with what they 'know to be true' from everyday experience.

A diagnostic teaching approach focuses on description and diagnosis of pupil misconceptions in terms of their responses to critical items, followed by remedial action. The remedial action takes the form of creating cognitive conflict between what they 'know to be true' and the result of their erroneous computation. This work, while interesting in itself, is discussed here because it illustrates the strong interdependence between teaching and assessment. It also shows how emphasis on understanding pupil attainment, linked with a willingness to experiment with different styles of teaching, can lead to a steady growth in knowledge about teaching and learning mathematics.

Diagnostic teaching is, perhaps, more radical than it first appears. Pupils are encouraged to make mistakes and are seduced into errors which they reflect upon and remediate for themselves or with teacher help. This approach is at variance with many common practices where errors are ignored or assigned to categories such as 'carelessness'. Several teaching experiments (some of which will be reviewed briefly here) suggest strongly that a diagnostic approach is superior to many other approaches, when the focus is to overcome pupil misconceptions. Discovering where misconceptions exist and analysing their sources are important skills for teachers to acquire. Things are made difficult because misconceptions, typically, do not give rise to poor performance overall, but rather inhibit perfect performance. Misconceptions are often revealed by predictable wrong responses to a few key items. From the teacher's viewpoint, a collection of such key items can be extremely useful, especially when associated with knowledge of likely underlying misconceptions and possible methods for remediation.

Experimenting in class

Teachers often experiment informally with a variety of teaching approaches. There is a good deal of scope within teaching for more formal experimental procedures. One can identify a number of aspects of diagnostic teaching, which can be evaluated separately. First one might compare the effects of teaching based on exposition of the correct methods and positive rewards for pupils, with an approach based on causing cognitive conflict in pupils' minds; a second theme could be the relationship between the amount and intensity of the discussion (which should be expected to be positively related to remediation) and pupil performance gains. A third might be to compare a diagnostic approach with an expository approach based on increasing pupils' understanding of the methods they are using. Bell *et al.* (1983), explored each of these issues in different contexts, namely, operations on decimals, use of directed quantities, and rates. In the first study, pupils' conceptions using decimals was explored. Tasks such as these were used.

1. Write down the next three terms in this sequence: 0.3; 0.6; 0.9; ...; ...; ...; (Adding on 0.3 each time).
2. Read this scale:

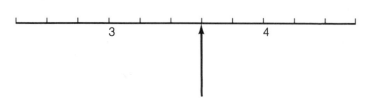

3. Which number has the largest value: 5.248, 5.4 or 5.63?

The positive only teaching approach focused on areas which were known to cause difficulty to pupils, and attempted to explain 'the correct way to do things' without any explicit discussion of misconceptions. The conflict approach began by exposing pupil misconceptions and then holding discussions, which would lead to the resolution of these misconceptions. There were clear and statistically significant gains for the group (taught by the same teacher) using the conflict method, both immediately after teaching and on a delayed post test.

A second study compared seven different classes who used similar teaching materials but which varied in the amount and intensity of the discussion involved in resolving the conflict. Directed quantities were studied. Typical problems were as follows.

1. 'Thriller' is up five places in the pop chart to number 8, where was it?
2. Last week a local shop sold 20 more records of 'Hello!' than it did this week. Last week 45 records were sold: how many were sold this week?
3. A woman went to the bank and asked to draw out £30 but the cashier said that would leave her £10 overdrawn. How much did she have in her account?

This study showed that the more vigorous and intense the discussions the greater the pupil gains.

Results from these and other studies suggest strongly that there are clear benefits to be gained from the unveiling of misconceptions by the analysis of pupil responses to key items, associated with teaching based on pupils explaining their conceptions (and misconceptions) clearly and evaluating them, defending them and modifying them via discussions with peers and discussions with their teacher. More passive forms of learning seem to be less effective.

From the teacher's viewpoint, there is a need to be vigilant in the whole domain of mathematics and to search for common (and less common) misconceptions that surround many topics which are taught. Collecting items which highlight misconceptions is a very useful activity. These can be used for quick diagnosis and when presented after remedial activities can give one a good idea of the extent to which pupils have overcome earlier misconceptions. The idea that pupils actively construe mathematics as they proceed is important. Extending knowledge of misconceptions and learning how to foster discussions which remediate these misconceptions is an obvious route to the growth of one's own skills.

An overview of diagnostic teaching

The thrust of the work on diagnostic teaching is not to identify small domains in mathematics where misconceptions have been identified clearly and where specific techniques exist for their remediation; rather the thrust is the methodology itself. The principles are summarized briefly below.

- To explore pupils' conceptions and misconceptions in detail;
- to develop items which highlight where these misconceptions exist;
- to find ways to encourage pupils to face up to their misconceptions and to explore actively the implications of their misconceptions (including discussions with their peers);
- to review the persistence of these misconceptions.

The examples which are available in the research literature are dramatic, exciting and give one the sense of control in the classroom when one recognizes similar patterns of errors in different pupils and when one can predict wrong answers that pupils will make, based on their answers to somewhat dissimilar questions. Nevertheless, as teachers, one's own learning should be focused not simply on the factual level concerning specific pupil misconceptions. Work needs to be done at higher order levels of learning how to diagnose misconceptions, in areas where the research literature has not yet started its explorations; and at the creative level of finding new methods to stimulate pupil reflection, and thereby to engineer cognitive conflict and remediation of misconceptions. Examples from work at the SCME on areas in which diagnostic explorations have been carried out can be provided to illustrate the breadth of the approach – i.e. to show that a diagnostic approach is not just appropriate to issues concerning simple number operations. Studies have been carried out on: misconceptions involving probability in sixth formers; notions of algebra; conversion between measures; ratio and proportion; and graphical interpretation in secondary school pupils; the naming and recognition of geometric shapes; place value; and counting on in primary school children. Of course, all the studies carried out by the CSMS project are relevant to the discussion of diagnostic skills. Those significant studies, indeed, were the trigger for many of the subsequent studies attempting to remediate the poor pupil performances reported. All the examples given show how much work there is yet to do both to identify misconceptions and to develop new activities to help pupils examine their constructions about mathematical topics for themselves. One's own classroom is probably an excellent place to begin extending this work!

Misconceptions have been treated as if they were capable of remediation almost in isolation from each other. There is a good deal yet to learn about misconceptions which cross subject boundaries (something is known about the problems of dealing with decimal quantities which transcend all areas where decimals are involved, for example). Little is known about the relative persistence of different misconceptions in the face of remedial activity, or which misconceptions are hardest to shift, or which misconceptions cluster together, or the long-term efficacy of remedial intervention. Any or all of these need classroom research. The work of the CSMS group (see Ridgway, 1988a for reviews) together with some of the packages developed for diagnostic teaching which are available from the SCME provide a good basis for your research (e.g. Bell, 1983).

Review

This chapter began by asking how results from standardized tests could be used in class. To answer the question, it was necessary to discover ways to describe what it is that tests measure. There is a need to demystify tests and to understand the nature of test items and to explain them to pupils. Descriptions of the tasks to be performed and analysis of pupil successes lead naturally to analyses of our personal successes and failures in class. More importantly, the task descriptions can form the basis for a discussion with pupils about some aspects of mathematical learning – for example by drawing attention to their relative strengths and weaknesses in different mathematical domains or processes. This emphasis on understanding the acquisition of mathematical knowledge and the need to remediate deficiencies and misconceptions led on to diagnostic teaching. This latter theme illustrated the intimate associations between teaching and testing.

The next section will pick up these themes again, albeit in a broader context. When psychometric tests are considered, the focus is usually on timed, written, rather short tasks. Teachers of mathematics have ambitions for pupil attainment which go way beyond such constraints. When one considers the requirements to provide new kinds of summative assessment for GCSE, it is clear that some broad statements about aims and objectives in mathematical education are needed. One needs to look for ways in which these aims and objectives can be crystallised in assessment tasks. The next section, therefore, will describe the new system of examination and the National Criteria for Mathematics, before examining ways in which some long dormant objectives can be awoken and converted to assessment tasks which might have a desirable 'backwash' effect on the curriculum, by stimulating many of Cockcroft's 'missing activities'.

Section B

4 New Systems of Examination

In England and Wales most pupils aged 16 years take externally moderated examinations to assess their attainment and to provide certification of attainment in a wide range of school subjects. Not all pupils take these examinations. Pupils at different levels of attainment take different examinations after following somewhat different courses of study. Before 1988 the two most commonly followed assessment schemes were provided by the General Certificate of Education (GCE) and the Certificate of Secondary Education (CSE). It was originally intended that GCE would be appropriate to assess the attainment of the most able 30 per cent of pupils, and that CSE would be used to assess the next 30 per cent of pupils. To allow comparability between GCE and CSE, a grade one pass at CSE was judged to be equivalent to a GCE pass. Several problems became apparent with this binary scheme.

The desire for comparability between a GCE pass and CSE grade one led to an increase in the CSE syllabus, both in terms of the domains covered, and in terms of difficulty level to be faced, with the result that a very wide range of topics, including some known to be difficult for pupils of average ability, e.g. algebra, were included. Examinations have a very powerful influence on what is taught in schools, and on how it is taught. Teachers often feel obliged to cover as much of the examination syllabus as they can. Before the introduction of GCSE, about 80 per cent of pupils in secondary school followed GCE or CSE courses in mathematics, despite the original intention to focus these examinations on the top 60 per cent of pupils. Course content was determined largely by the likely attainments of the most able 25 per cent (i.e., those likely to pass GCE). It followed therefore, that the bulk of students were faced with mathematical tasks way beyond their abilities.

This was reflected in the performance levels which were recorded. For example, at CSE, a grade four corresponded to a candidate being awarded about 30 per cent of the available marks, and a grade five ('the performance just below that to be expected from a pupil of average ability') was awarded to a pupil who obtained about 20 per cent of the available marks.

What were the implications of this situation for pupils of average attainment? Educationally, it is quite undesirable for pupils to be faced with tasks which they are aware they are unable to perform. However, teachers felt obliged to prepare students for these examinations, and therefore often provided intellectual challenges in class which pupils could not meet. As a result pupils lacked confidence in their mathematical skills, and disliked the subject. It is not surprising that the mathematical competence of adults is as poor as reported in surveys such as those carried out by Bridgid Sewell (1981). Teachers who wished to give their pupils some chance of success in the examination were likely to adopt a teaching style which attempted to foster mathematical technique at the expense of mathematical understanding.

The Cockcroft committee suggested that lower attaining pupils should face less demanding mathematical challenges and should be expected to achieve far higher levels of success. They argued that pupils would be far better off being equipped with a range of lower level mathematical skills which they have mastered and understood, than with a few loose ideas about some skills which are harder to acquire, and which they are quite unable to use reliably.

A further problem with GCE and CSE was associated with the multiplicity of syllabuses available – there were 17 different GCE mathematics syllabuses, for example. In 1986, there were nine Examination Boards for the GCE (GCE Boards), and 13 Examination Boards for the CSE (CSE Boards). The examination boards work autonomously and are financed largely by examination entry fees paid by LEAs. Schools could choose which GCE Board they liked, but were obliged, in general, to enter pupils for examinations set by their regional CSE Board. One virtue of the multiplicity of examination syllabuses was that teachers could select a syllabus well suited to the needs of their pupils. Conversely, there were problems associated with the transfer of pupils between a CSE course and a GCE course if early decisions about appropriate schemes of study were wrong.

GCE and CSE both used a system of norm-referencing to allocate grades to candidates. Broadly speaking, grade boundaries were determined initially by dividing the score distribution up on some a priori basis – for example the top 10 per cent of candidates might be awarded a Grade A, the next 10 per cent a Grade B, the next 10 per cent a Grade C, and so on. Such a system is 'fair' if large numbers of candidates are tested each year, and if the overall standards do not vary greatly from year to year. When these conditions hold, candidates in different years who have the same grade are likely to have performed equally well. Norm-referenced tests are useful for the purposes of selection for employment, or for entry into higher education. The major task of such selection systems might be better described as 'rejection' – the main task is to find a way of denying access to the bulk of applicants on some apparently rational basis (since the number of university places, for example, is fixed, and small compared to student demand). Of course, the design and grading of national examinations was not as mindless as this description suggests. The content of the examinations was related to the content of the courses which pupils followed, and syllabuses were designed with some educational goals in mind. Consequently, although examination results gave no direct information about the specific competence of candidates, they did give a crude idea of their successes in a loosely defined area of skills such as 'mathematics' or 'English literature'. A further problem was that two candidates with the same examination grade might have demonstrated quite different competences, because most examinations allowed candidates some choice in the questions they attempted. The examinations, therefore, were unlike psychometric tests which ask all candidates to attempt all aspects of the test in order to obtain an overall picture of abilities – examinations failed to sample the pupils' knowledge across the breadth of the curriculum. It was hard, therefore, for parents and employers to know what had been learnt, since grades reflected standards relative to other pupils who had taken the examination, and were not descriptions of the tasks which pupils could perform.

The examination system before 1988 was not remorselessly tied to norm-referencing; one of the important tasks of Boards of Examiners was always to set grade boundaries based, not only on a consideration of the score distribution obtained on the examinations, but also on the grounds of qualitative judgements about the overall level of performance. So GCE and CSE examination grades were not allocated on the basis of rigid adherence to a particular statistical model. Nevertheless, judgements about the quality of examination performance, and the setting of grade boundaries were not based on a specification of clear criteria; rather they were based on qualitative judgements which were rarely made explicit.

In an attempt to solve the problems identified above, namely a multiplicity of syllabuses and examination boards, problems of comparability between GCE and CSE, problems of transfer of course of study between GCE and CSE, curricula geared to the needs of the most able which are quite unsuited to the needs of the majority of pupils, and normative versus criterion-referenced performance, a new form of examination was introduced in 1988. The overall responsibility for the new GCSE rests with the Examination Groups and the Secondary Examinations Council (SEC). One goal of the GCSE is to provide a single system of assessment, which will eventually make explicit statements about what pupils have attained, via the construction of a system of criteria-related grades.

The introduction of the GCSE required the amalgamation of the CSE and GCE Boards into five Regional Examination Groups who administer the new examination; schools are free to decide which examinations their pupils will take.

GCSE provides a common examination framework to replace the old binary system of GCE and CSE. The relationship between the boundaries of the grades obtained on each system is illustrated in Figure 4.1 below.

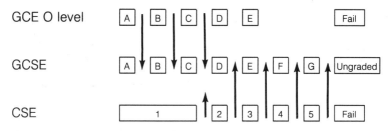

Figure 4.1: The relationship between CSE, GCE and GCSE

The SEC and the examination groups have issued a set of National Criteria which are the product of extensive consultation within the educational community on 'the educational purposes and character of the subject within schools, colleges and examination boards'.

The purposes of the National Criteria are to set out, 'in varying degrees of detail, the aims, assessment objectives, content and broad assessment patterns which will form the basis for the new GCSE syllabuses'. The new GCSE syllabuses in twenty 'majority subjects' were submitted to the SEC for approval, to ensure that all aspects of assessment are consistent with these National Criteria.

The Secondary Examinations Council together with the Joint Council for the GCSE (the GCSE Groups forum) is responsible for keeping the National Criteria under review. The terms of the general criteria state that the National Criteria will be monitored and amended as necessary so as to take account of promising innovations in syllabus matters.

The National Criteria, of course, are less detailed than an examination syllabus, and are therefore far less detailed than a teaching syllabus. While the criteria describe content, at least as important are statements of aims defined for GCSE courses and the behavioural objectives that examinations are required to assess. There was a clear intention to introduce a wider variety of methods of assessment in order to bring about a wider variety of classroom practice, and to reward a far wider range of mathematical attainments than could be rewarded by timed written examinations of the sort commonly used in GCE mathematics. GCSE represents an important historical change in the role of examinations in education in the UK; it is the first large scale attempt to use the examination system to steer the curriculum in desirable directions.

Full criterion-referencing is almost certain to be impossible in practice because of the problems of specifying tasks in a completely unambiguous manner. Nevertheless, a movement from conventional norm-referencing towards an attempt to specify the nature of the skills that have been acquired is undoubtedly a good thing, so long as we recognize and avoid the danger that those aspects of mathematical attainment which are easy to set criteria for (notably low level, factual and technical skills) might come to dominate the curriculum, at the expense of equally valuable skills concerned with problem solving and mathematical operations in open environments, simply because the latter are rather harder to define and assess. The aim of the SEC is to identify some of the competences in which candidates need to demonstrate 'mastery'. Of course, the definition of 'mastery' is not altogether clear either. It would be impractical to expect candidates to attain perfect scores on every aspect of every task on which they were tested – which would be necessary in a system which reflects a true definition of criterion-referencing to mastery levels. So the SEC is faced with a task of making decisions about the level of success which counts for mastery, and also the number of criteria which must be satisfied in order for a candidate to obtain a particular grade. There is a clear intention that criteria be expressed in positive terms and reflect a candidate's competences, rather than incompetences. At lower grades this involves the assessment of skills which in GCE and CSE days might have been judged to be too elementary to examine and certify.

A major problem arises when one seeks to satisfy the educational needs of the most able and least able pupils within the same examination system; this problem is highlighted by the 'seven year gap'. A task that can be performed by an 11-year-old pupil of average ability can also be performed by highly able seven-year-olds, but not by low attaining 14-year-olds. This is illustrated in the test score norms of almost every test considered in *A Review of Mathematics Tests* (see Table 2.3 for example); when one examines the difference in mean raw score between pupils whose ages are 12 months apart, it is usually quite small compared to the difference in raw score between pupils of the same age, but at the 15th and 85th percentiles.

In GCE and CSE examinations, marks across the range of student ability usually produced a Normal (i.e., bell-shaped) score distribution, as shown by curves (a) and (b) of Figure 4.2. Grade boundaries were not set in advance (so 60 per cent was not 'Grade B'); rather, they were established by a mixture of statistical technique (since it is very easy to divide the scores up into any number of segments of specified proportions – 10 per cent of pupils might be given grade A etc.) and examiners' judgement, which was based on knowledge of performance in earlier years, on the difficulty of the questions, and on judgements about samples of examination scripts located near the borders of examination grades.

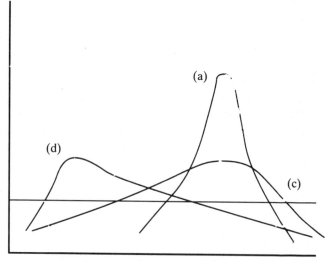

Figure 4.2:   Possible GCE and CSE score distributions

For the same measurement reliability, judgements about candidate grades are made easier if the spread of scores is greater – so it is easier to set grade boundaries on score distribution (b) than on (a). Obviously, if very small differences in marks lead to large differences in obtained grades then small fluctuations in candidate performance on the day of examination or in marker standards can have unjustifiably large effects on grades allocated to individuals. For the purposes of discriminating between individuals who attain pass grades, a flat distribution of candidates across scores in the pass range is desirable, as illustrated by curve (c). This distribution is also very difficult to achieve in practice! However, score distributions like (d) in Figure 4.2 can be achieved, if the difficulty level of questions is carefully matched to the abilities of the pupils being examined. Examples of psychometric tests with score distributions like (d) in Figure 4.2 were provided by *Moray House Junior Mathematics Tests 2 and 10*, (now out of print) which were designed to help allocation of pupils to secondary schools in LEAs which still provide selective education. This distribution of marks would be quite inappropriate for GCSE, given the demands for positive pupil attainment. It is far easier to produce such a score distribution for psychometric tests which are made up of a large number of compulsory items, each of which has a known difficulty level for the target group, established via large scale testing on representative pupil samples, than it is to produce such a score distribution for an examination on which pupils select a small number of questions, none of which have been piloted to establish their difficulty levels.

Consider the problems created by the demands for a single examination which must discriminate amongst the most able 60–70 per cent of pupils, using seven pass grades on which the bulk of candidates should score 60 per cent or more of the marks available. The ability range of the pupils is very large, and all the pupils must achieve a high degree of success. Yet the examination paper must also have the power to discriminate amongst the candidates. These contradictory demands cannot be satisfied by a single examination. They might be satisfied by a system of carefully developed examination papers, each one targetted to discriminate between pupils of different abilities. The Cockcroft committee, therefore, proposed a system of differentiated levels of assessment in order to cater for the widely differing range of pupil attainment found. This is illustrated in Figure 4.3.

Broadly, two schemes of assessment have been proposed. One is based on a system of four papers, the other is based on three pairs of parallel papers. In both schemes papers are available which differ in

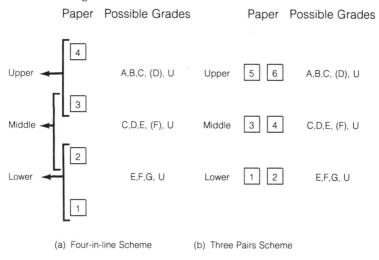

(a) Four-in-line Scheme   (b) Three Pairs Scheme

Figure 4.3:   Possible schemes of assessment of GCSE

terms of increasing breadth of syllabus and increasing difficulty. So in the four paper scheme, paper 4 contains more mathematical topics, and also deals with each in greater depth. Pupils will be permitted to take no more than two papers. Since grades can only be awarded on the basis of positive achievement, poor performance on a difficult paper will not lead to the award of a much lower grade; rather it will lead to no award at all. So a candidate who takes Papers 3 and 4 on the four-in-line scheme can only expect to get grades A, B, C, D, or be ungraded, and so on. Details of the schemes used by each Examination Group are shown in Appendix 1. An example of how the difficulty level of four papers might be set so as to provide good discrimination between candidates, while ensuring a good examination performance by all, is given in Figure 4.4.

On this scheme it is important that candidates be entered for examinations at an appropriate level; candidates who are likely to obtain middle or lower grades would be ill-advised to enter for paper four, for example. In general, one would expect teachers to be skilled at making assessments about the appropriate level at which pupils are to be entered. In order to help pupils, it is necessary to resist pressure both from pupils and parents to enter pupils for papers at a higher level than estimates of pupil competence would suggest – such pressures can probably be best resisted by explaining the structure of the examinations. Some guidance, of course, will be provided from the coursework which pupils complete as part of their overall assessment. It is hoped that

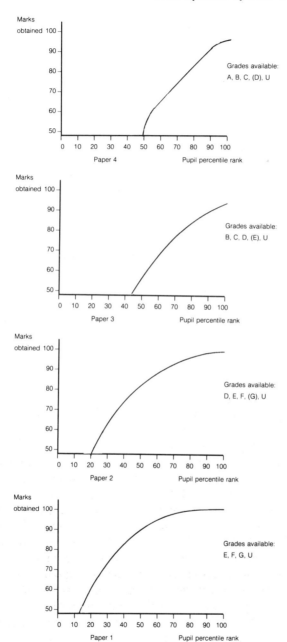

Figure 4.4:   Possible mark distributions

students will be entered at a level at which they will meet questions which are well within their own reach. If this is achieved, then pupils will no longer find themselves faced with mathematical tasks which are way beyond their competence, and teachers will not be required to attempt to equip them to face such tasks via technical drill.

In this discussion of 'marks obtained', we must distinguish between pupils feelings that they have done well, and demonstrated their knowledge and skills, and the actual marks obtained. For example, on problems which consist of a number of parts, success on earlier easier parts can give pupils a feeling of achievement, even if this achievement is not rewarded heavily by the marking scheme, compared with performance on harder later parts, such as 'explain why your pattern works'; or 'generalize this result to three-dimensional objects'. Issues of marking will be considered later.

Clearly this new system is intended to produce a differentiated curriculum, better suited to the abilities of all pupils. Lower attaining pupils will proceed more slowly, and face tasks appropriate to their needs, whilst higher attaining pupils will proceed to a wider range of topics which they will tackle in a more sophisticated fashion – for example meeting algebra, notions of proof, and the like. The intention is to provide a range of intellectual challenges that are well suited to individual needs – lower attaining pupils will make positive progress, and higher attaining pupils will meet intellectual challenges which they cannot just 'coast through'. Lower levels are completely contained within higher levels, and so pupils who vary markedly in the rate at which they acquire mathematical skills (for example 'late developers') need not be consigned at an early stage to a fixed track, suitable only for lower attaining pupils. The levels are intended to be 'upward compatible' to use computer jargon.

GCSE is designed to present pupils with tasks which they are able to perform with relative ease. It is not an attempt to present them with very difficult tasks which they make a poor attempt at. Progress is being made towards specifying grade-related criteria; in the short term there is a clear emphasis on positive attainment such as, 'Sanjay can multiply single digit whole numbers accurately, and can add fractions whose denominators are 2, 4, and 8', rather than 'Sanjay gets about 20 per cent of the marks on some hard maths questions we have developed'.

Will this scheme of assessment be able to meet these laudable objectives? Considerable problems are posed in the four-in-line model by having only four papers to distinguish the abilities of a very wide range of candidates. Since each pupil will take two adjacent papers, paper three will be taken by about two-thirds of the candidature, (as will paper two) since it will be taken by all candidates who also take paper four and paper two. (Papers one and three in the case of paper two). The design of an examination paper which is suitable for the needs of such a large sample of pupils – given the very wide range of pupil attainments noted earlier – will be problematic. There is a clear need for questions which differ in difficulty, or for questions which are sectioned in such a way that later parts present increasingly difficult challenges after relatively straightforward earlier ones.

One approach is to present an examination paper in which easier questions are presented at the beginning and harder ones towards the end. A second strategy is to design questions in such a way that later parts present increasingly difficult challenges. One might doubt the wisdom implicit in both strategies of having a system in which lower attaining pupils gain their marks via a series of short questions, or by attempting the early parts of a large number of harder questions. It is quite undesirable for lower attaining pupils to demonstrate competence via fragmentary performance on a wide range of mathematical tasks, and more able ones to demonstrate competence via complete performance on a few integrated tasks.

At the time of writing (December, 1987) there is already evidence that certain Examination Boards will give low pass grades for poor performance on harder papers. They are wrong to do so. Such actions are likely to have a strong negative backwash effect on classroom practice.

Towards a national curriculum 5–16

The introduction of GCSE is part of a government initiative to introduce a national curriculum in maintained schools in England and Wales. Mathematics will form part of the core curriculum (along with science and English). It is claimed that a number of benefits will be associated with the introduction of a national curriculum. These include the following.

- Increased continuity in children's education (for example between primary and secondary school, or for pupils who move schools at any stage in their education);
- a better curriculum will be followed in some schools, than at present;

- increasing the accountability of schools to parents, governors and LEAs, and the Secretaries of State;
- making the school curriculum intelligible to pupils and parents;
- raised standards of pupil attainment.

Standards will be raised by the following.

- Ensuring that all pupils follow a broad and balanced range of school subjects, up to the age of 16;
- defining achievement objectives for pupils of different levels of ability; these objectives will be communicated to each pupil, and will then act as challenges for the pupils, his or her parents, and teachers to tackle;
- monitoring pupil performance to ensure that progress is being maintained and that appropriate achievement objectives are being set;
- communicating pupil performance to parents, together with information on the range of classmarks;
- ensuring that all pupils 'have access to the same... programmes of study which include the key content, skills and processes which they need to learn...';
- enabling governors, the headteacher and teachers to review the effectiveness of their own school, taking account of both local circumstances, and the national attainment patterns;
- allowing for more detailed monitoring of pupil performance, to identify individuals with particular educational needs.

A National Curriculum Council (NCC) will be appointed to advise the Secretary of State on matters concerned with the national curriculum in schools. This body will replace the School Curriculum Development Committee (SCDC), and will be 'an essential means of securing a properly founded national curriculum' and will review the national curriculum and offer the Secretary of State advice on appropriate means for its maintenance and improvement. The NCC will establish a working group on mathematics and will consult with interested groups on that group's recommendations on attainment targets and programmes of study.

A School Examinations and Assessment Council (SEAC) will be appointed in 1989 which will replace the Secondary Examinations Council. SEAC is likely to be responsible for:

- advising the Secretaries of State about the criteria appropriate for syllabuses and examinations;

- approving syllabuses and examinations which lead to public qualifications;
- establishing procedures for distributing national tests and other means of assessment, and moderating schools' assessments (usually via contracts with the GCSE examining groups); monitoring the efficacy of national tests and other forms of assessment, and advising the Secretaries of State appropriately. It is intended that the new schemes will be capable of being rapidly updated on the basis of experience in use;
- liaising with the National Council for Vocational Qualifications (NCVQ) to ensure coherence between vocational and school-based qualifications.

A task group on Assessment and Testing (TGAT) has been established to offer advice on methods of assessment which are affordable and easy to understand and use. It is hoped that a consistent approach will be used by all of the subject working groups. The tasks of the mathematics working group are to:

- outline the contribution of mathematics to the school curriculum;
- outline programmes of study appropriate to pupils of different levels of ability in compulsory education. These programmes will set out 'the overall content, knowledge, skills and processes relevant to today's needs' which pupils should be taught;
- outline attainment targets appropriate to pupils of different levels of ability, which relate to the programmes of study, and which can be assessed at different ages, likely to be seven, 11, 14 and 16 years.

The programmes of study and definitions of attainment should take account of current good practice, together with relevant research, and work on curriculum development. It is suggested that the national criteria for GCSE mathematics can provide the basis for assessment at age 16 and for programmes of study to ages 14–16. In addition, the potential for cross-curricular links should be explored.

The working group will be expected to determine attainment targets which tests will assess, but will not be responsible for the development of assessment methods themselves. That work will be carried out by organizations which have already demonstrated their competence in the domain of test production, who will follow guidelines established by TGAT. The Assessment of Performance Unit (APU) of the Department of Education and Science (DES)

will help direct the test development programme. This development programme will not be confined exclusively to the production
of national tests, but will also develop tests which teachers can use
for the purposes of internal assessment as and when they see fit. It is
intended that a bank of tests will be constructed, which will include
a number of tests already in existence.

This plan for a national curriculum, supported by regular national
tests, represents a dramatic innovation in educational practice in
England and Wales. It will require extensive work on curriculum
development, test design, and teacher education. The definition of
the curriculum, the attainment targets, and the assessment tests will
be of crucial importance to its success. The mathematics working
group is due to report in the summer of 1988, and so, at the time of
writing, no comments can be made concerning either the attainment targets or the assessment tasks. The dangers of an undesirable
backwash effect induced by inappropriate tests were described
earlier. Hopefully these will be avoided by the plan to design
assessment tasks which reflect curriculum intentions, and the
general strategy being employed, namely using assessment to drive
the curriculum. Nevertheless, an emphasis on tests which are
'affordable' and externally moderated is likely to result in paper and
pencil tests which are easy to mark, and which are likely therefore to
fail to assess practical skills, problem solving, investigative work, or
group work, all of which are essential elements of mathematics
curricula. Undesirable effects are likely if these externally moderated tests achieve a public eminence not enjoyed by school and
teacher moderated assessments.

A second danger is that teacher, departmental, and school
autonomy is likely to be reduced quite significantly by the introduction of a national curriculum. The long term effects of a shift in the
role of teachers as transmitters of a curriculum designed by others is
hard to assess, but is unlikely to be welcomed by teachers
themselves.

The relationship between national tests developed under con-
tract to the design of the mathematics working group, marked by
teachers and moderated by examination boards, and GCSE, set and
marked by examination boards, is unclear at present.

Towards more varied mathematics

The National Criteria emphasize that new schemes of assessment
must involve oral assessments, mental calculations, practical and

investigational work, and will require pupils to undertake extended pieces of work. Obviously these requirements cannot be met by the old GCE format of timed written examinations. Coursework assessment has long been an integral part of CSE work and hopefully CSE experiences will form a base on which newer methods of assessment can be built. By 1991 all GCSE syllabuses in mathematics will include assessment in each of the above areas and will contain a substantial element of coursework. Correspondingly in the period between 1988 and 1990 Examining Groups will be working to provide schemes of assessment aimed at satisfying these two criteria. Coursework elements are likely to be significant and will contribute between 20 per cent and 50 per cent of the total assessment. The National Criteria allow considerable freedom in the way in which assessment methods are devised to meet these new criteria. In the intervening period up to 1991 Examining Groups will, it is hoped, explore a wide variety of novel methods of assessment and will share their expertise each with the other. This intervening period will allow teachers time to acclimatise themselves to new methods of working and of assessing a wider variety of mathematical attainments. No doubt many teachers will take advantage of the opportunity to include new components in their pupils' assessment on a 'voluntary' basis in the period 1988–90.

Each Examination Group will decide on the nature of the coursework set, the way it is to be examined and moderated, and the weight it will be given overall. Details of the schemes devised by each group, as far as they were known in November 1986 are shown in Appendix 1.

Overview of assessment

The introduction of the GCSE was a direct attempt to produce examination driven curriculum change. The intended direction of change is towards a broadening of the range of mathematical skills which pupils learn, associated with a broader ranged teaching and learning style in class. In order to sample a wider range of skills, GCSE will provide a balance of techniques for assessment which cover both written aspects and other aspects including practical work, investigations, mental mathematics, and oral work. Assessment within each of these areas may well be unfamiliar to teachers, and will require careful preparation. It is clear from the National Criteria that coursework must be seen to complement written examinations, and the degree of overlap between the two need not be great. There is little to be gained by assessing exactly the same kinds of mathematical attainment in both the coursework and the timed written component of the assessment.

Many people view the move away from timed written examinations to more open forms of assessment as a threat. The change might be seen as introducing subjective elements into procedures which were more objective beforehand. Teachers may have qualms about their own abilities to assess new kinds of mathematics. The prospect of monitoring such things as pupils' ability to interact in groups, to carry out practical tasks, and to do investigations might seem to lead into areas of mathematical activity which have scarcely been considered before. Conversely, there is a rising awareness that timed written examinations have many limitations as the sole basis for assessment. In other countries, such as West Germany, far more emphasis is placed on teacher assessments of pupils, and there the idea of externally moderated examinations is viewed with a good deal of suspicion.

One must also be careful not to confuse high reliability with high validity. Consensus between markers does not necessarily mean that what is being asessed is the pupil's mathematical attainment. Two distinct issues are involved in such judgements. The first is whether the range of questions chosen reflects the curriculum studied (clearly examination boards have a major responsibility here) and whether pupil performance on these tasks reflects their ability to perform them. The second question is the extent to which timed written examinations can sample the wide range of mathematical skills which pupils possess. Lower reliability need not be a retrograde step, especially if increased validity is bought at the expense of this reduced reliability. In subjects such as English, where essay marking is common, concerns about the subjective elements involved in marking essays are rarely raised. There, high reliability could easily be obtained by making the assessment process a matter of multiple choice questions on tasks concerned with grammar or vocabulary. However, both of these would be judged to involve knowledge too narrow for a valid measure of ability in English, and would therefore hardly be entertained. In mathematics it is essential to make judgements about tasks considered to be valid indicators of mathematical attainment. The National Criteria, which are considered in the next chapter, offer good starting points. Striving for some increased reliability once these valid tasks have been determined is important, but establishing reliability as a major goal and ignoring validity would be folly.

5 Examining the National Criteria

This chapter offers a brief guide to the GCSE National Criteria for Mathematics.

The National Criteria set out '*essential* requirements which *must* be satisfied by all syllabuses for examinations entitled Mathematics' (my italics). The role of the SEC as a monitor of Examination Groups' attempts to satisfy the National Criteria represents an important historical change in educational practice at this level.

The acknowledgement that examinations influence classroom practice is not new; however, the idea of using the examination system to produce better classroom practice via examination driven curricula has only ever been tried before on a very small scale.

Aims

The National Criteria are derived to a large extent from discussions and recommendations proposed in the Cockcroft Report. The aims place a welcome emphasis on oral and practical skills, and describe the need for pupils to read and talk about mathematics, as well as the ubiquitous written skills. Achieving these aims will require a major shift in the ways mathematics is taught; assessing them will require radical departures from current practices.

Demands that pupils 'apply mathematics in everyday situations', and 'develop an understanding of the part which mathematics plays in the world around them' are yet more problematic.

The aims emphasize the need for pupils to:

- solve problems, check their results, and present solutions clearly;
- understand mathematical principles;
- model situations mathematically when it is appropriate to do

so (especially in a cognate domain such as science and technology);
- express themselves clearly, using mathematics;
- reason logically;
- prove and generalize;
- classify, and appreciate patterns and relationships;
- develop an awareness of aesthetics in mathematics by producing creative and imaginative work;
- experiment and inquire and investigate;
- work collaboratively;
- see the interconnected nature of mathematics; and
- acquire a foundation for further study.

The statement of aims would certainly have been judged as idealistic as little as 10 years ago. They show the change in intellectual climate that has taken place which is, in part, attributable to the Cockcroft Report. Not only are idealistic statements being made, they are also being treated seriously within the community associated with mathematical education.

Assessment objectives

The assessment objectives provide clearer guidance about which of the aims can and should be assessed directly, and offer guidance about appropriate kinds of assessment.

Assessment objectives define processes and qualities, as well as abilities and skills, and are therefore radically different from traditional definitions which have focused on descriptions of content. 'Any scheme of assessment will test the ability of candidates to:

3.1   recall, apply and interpret mathematical knowledge in the context of everyday situations;...'

The decision to set mathematics in a familiar context is welcome, even though the use of 'everyday situations' can be problematic. Difficulties will be discussed in a later chapter on *Assessing Practical Work in Mathematics*.

'3.2   set out mathematical work, including the solution of problems, in a logical and clear form using appropriate symbols and terminology;

3.3 organise, interpret and present information, accurately in written, tabular, graphical and diagrammatic forms'.

The first objective is straightforward; the second, however, asks not only for organization and presentation of information in a variety of forms (which might be considered to be examples of exercising technical skills) but also for interpretation. This requirement for conceptual analysis and understanding places new demands on assessment procedures. One would be hard-pressed to assess pupils' ability to interpret information without recourse to essay-style responses. While almost every subject other than mathematics asks for, and assesses such contributions quite routinely, essays engender fears amongst mathematics examiners about the subjectivity and the unreliability of judgements being made. Reliability does not plummet simply because pupils are allowed to make open-ended responses; rather, more training is required to make reliable judgements, and more time is needed for examiners to make such judgements than Examination Boards usually allow.

'3.4 perform calculations by suitable methods;
3.5 use an electronic calculator;
3.6 understand systems of measurement in everyday use and make use of them in the solution of problems;
3.7 estimate, approximate and work to degrees of accuracy appropriate to the context;
3.8 use mathematical and other instruments to measure and draw to an acceptable degree of accuracy.'

The above objectives focus on a range of useful, practical skills in mathematics. Particularly welcome is the inclusion of the use of a calculator as an assessment objective. It is unfortunate, however, that no reference is made to the use of computers. One might trace some historical reasons why this is the case (including the brief though damning comments in the Cockcroft Report). Dramatic educational advances have been made in the use of computers in mathematical education, and the use of computers should, in my view, be an assessment objective. Supporting arguments can be found in the Council for Educational Technology report (1987), *Will Mathematics Count?*

The task of working 'to degrees of accuracy appropriate to the context' demands that pupils must acquire a sophisticated view of measurement, and must relate technical issues to conceptual ones.

'3.9 recognise patterns and structures in a variety of situations, and form generalisations;

3.10 interpret, transform and make appropriate use of mathematical statements expressed in words or symbols;

3.11 recognise and use spatial relationships in two and three dimensions, particularly in solving problems;

3.12 analyse a problem, select a suitable strategy and apply an appropriate technique to obtain its solution;

3.13 apply combinations of mathematical skills and techniques in problem solving;

3.14 make logical deductions from given mathematical data;

3.15 respond to a problem relating to a relatively unstructured situation by translating it into an appropriately structured form.'

Each of the above objectives emphasises the need to develop problem solving skills of a general nature. This focus on the process aspects of mathematics represents an intended shift in favour of more open styles of teaching and learning mathematics. Approaches to the assessment and teaching of such skills will be described in the following chapter.

'Two further assessment objectives can be fully realised only by assessing work carried out by candidates in addition to time-limited written examinations. From 1988 to 1990 all Examining Groups must provide at least one scheme which includes some elements of these two objectives. From 1991 these objectives must be realised fully in all schemes.

3.16 respond orally to questions about mathematics, discuss mathematical ideas and carry out mental calculations.

3.17 carry out practical and investigational work, and undertake extended pieces of work.'

Oral work, mental arithmetic, practical work and the conduct of investigations and projects must all be assessed by 1991 at the latest. The intervening period is intended to allow everyone, notably teachers and examiners, to learn how to conduct these activites – found to be conspicuously absent in the 1979 HMI Survey – and how to assess them.

Before attempting an overview of the National Criteria, one interesting omission should be noticed. Nowhere does it say that examination questions should have time limits.

Overview of the National Criteria

The whole notion of the criterion-referencing of process skills and conceptual understanding is problematic. Objectives which use words and phrases like 'interpret', 'understand', 'form generalizations', 'select a suitable strategy', 'discuss mathematical ideas' cannot be considered to be criteria in the sense implied by 'criterion-referenced testing'. While these are all desirable objectives, they do not say what it is that pupils who have satisfied such criteria have been able to do. A large set of exemplary tasks will need to be defined before the meaning of these objectives becomes clear. Until these tasks are available to specify performance criteria, the National Criteria should be thought of as the National Aims and Objectives.

The assessment objectives will place a much wider range of demands on pupils, teachers and examiners. The emphasis on coursework raises problems about how it will be set, marked and moderated. In general, there is a need to develop marking schemes which focus on qualitative judgements of pupil performance; it is extremely unlikely that marking schemes based on an atomistic description of performance can be developed e.g., '3 marks for method; 1 mark for accuracy' which will be suitable for all assessment needs.

No Examining Group has expertise in this new domain; it is almost certain that examination questions will need to be trialled on pupils who will not be taking a particular group's examinations, so that informed judgements can be made about the difficulty of questions, and so that Chief Examiners have sets of scripts on which to base (and evaluate) new forms of marking. The APU, the National Foundation for Educational Research (NFER) and CSMS projects have extensive data on some item difficulties for the target population, albeit on a rather narrower range of questions than those implied by the National Criteria. Such data will probably be valuable to groups in their early attempts to set new kinds of examination.

The list of objectives includes some which are obviously well suited to coursework (e.g. investigations, projects) and others which have been examined via timed, written examinations in the past. Judgements need to be made about which forms of assessment are best suited to which objectives. It would be clear violation of the aims set out in the National Criteria if written examinations focused exclusively on the assessment of facts and skills, and coursework dealt with conceptual structures, and general strategies. If coursework (including oral mathematics, practical work, projects, and investigations) receives little weight in the overall scheme, then the intentions underlying the new GCSE scheme will have been thwarted, and the new scheme need be little better than the one which it replaced.

Examination Groups face considerable problems. Examiners are used to rigidly applied, easy to use marking schemes; these will generally be inapplicable for GCSE. Examiners will have to be trained to use new schemes. It may well be worth adopting the practices employed by the APU for marking, until the examiners working for groups have acquired more expertise. The APU procedure, as well as having training sessions and standardization meetings, is to provide pupil scripts which are used to establish marking criteria. As well as these scripts, examiners are expected to refer all difficult cases up to more senior markers. Groups will probably also have to pay markers more.

The Examination Groups have a major responsibility to explain and defend the new styles of examination question which they will employ, and to advocate new styles of teaching. It is inadequate to point teachers to the National Criteria, or to send out leaflets describing syllabus changes. Information must be offered to teachers in a variety of ways, so that representative teachers get to hear and believe that things will be different. Lots of exemplars of questions, together with marking schemes which show those aspects of pupil performance which are most valued, need to be provided. The chapters that follow offer some suggestions on appropriate assessment schemes, and point to teaching resources which can help teachers develop appropriate pupil skills. Chapters focus on problem solving, investigations, group work, and the assessment of practical work in mathematics.

6 A Precursor to GCSE: the TSS Project

In 1981, the Shell Centre for Mathematical Education (SCME) established a project to explore the testing of strategic skills. Strategic skills are those skills which enable one to face, and make progress on unfamiliar tasks. (Some of these skills will be itemized later.) Early in the project, it became clear that the development of tests for the assessment of such abilities (supposing such tests could be produced) is rather peripheral to the major tasks of mathematical education, namely fostering pupils' strategic skills. Even a cursory examination of the publications of the Association of Teachers of Mathematics (ATM) or the Mathematical Association (MA) reveals a range of resources devoted to the promotion of problem solving in class; problem solving activities are strongly advocated by both associations. Nevertheless, the Secondary Survey, carried out in 1979 by Her Majesty's Inspectorate of Schools (HMI) revealed that problem solving, investigation, practical work, and discussion are all 'missing activities' in mathematics classes in secondary schools. How can this be the case?

An analysis of the educational system within which individual mathematics lessons take place leads to the conclusion that the dominant influence on classroom practice is the externally moderated examinations which pupils face at the age of 16. If any progress was to be made in fostering strategic skills as a routine activity in a large number of mathematics classrooms, then the external examinations would have to reward such activities, otherwise very few teachers would devote precious classroom time to them. While this idea is now widely accepted, it was viewed as being somewhat radical, then. Fortunately, the publication of the Cockcroft Report in 1982 gave it instant credibility. The mathematics subject committee of the Joint Matriculation Board (JMB) agreed to explore the possibility of introducing new kinds of questions into its O-level examination papers. Examination Boards have to serve the best interests of children and teachers (rather than those of academic researchers) and must proceed with due care. The research team therefore wrote a strong set of objections to an examination driven curriculum and set out to defuse them, via empirical research which would convince a reasonable sceptic. The objections set out were that:

- examiners can't examine process skills;
- teachers can't teach them; and
- pupils can't learn them.

These statements are meant to apply to the clients of Examination Boards – i.e. representative teachers and pupils, rather than exceptional ones. Subsequent research focused on the development of classroom materials for pupils and teachers, teacher support materials, and examination questions. Collaboration with groups of expert teachers has been a characteristic of all this research; so, too, has been emphasis on extensive classroom trialling and observation of material in use, and radical revision of materials in the light of these observations. The outcome from this research was a carefully developed package of materials which supported a variety of 'missing activities' and which fostered the acquisition of strategic skills. The first package – Problems with Patterns and Numbers, Joint Matriculation Board/Shell Centre for Mathematical Education (1984) (PPN or 'the Blue Box') comprises:

1. a 168 page Module Book, whose contents include: an introduction to the module; specimen examination questions, accompanied by marking schemes, and illustrated with sample pupil scripts; lesson plans to support classroom materials; general support materials which offer suggestions for cooperative activities within the mathematics department such as the analysis of lessons presented on video tape, group problem solving, and use of the microcomputer;
2. a set of photocopy 'masters' for: classroom materials, teacher-group support materials; specimen examination questions; marked and unmarked answers; and assessment sheets;
3. a videotape illustrating something of the variety of teaching styles that can be employed when using the materials, together with explanatory notes;
4. a computer disk containing five programs, together with explanatory notes.

The JMB introduced a revision of their O-level syllabus in 1984, which took effect in 1986, eliminating some syllabus elements. A new question was introduced on the 1986 paper, aimed at assessing pupils' ability to deal with less familiar problems which involved patterns and numbers. No new syllabus content was introduced because the existing description already identified relevant skills in general terms, even though no specific attempts had previously been made to assess them.

Thus, the JMB, with the assistance of the SCME, embarked on a programme of examination driven, modular change to the mathematics curriculum. Although small in scale (each module accounting for about five per cent of the syllabus), the changes were radical – aiming to foster strategic skills, and to stimulate many of the missing activities identified in the Cockcroft Report. A question relevant to The Language of Functions and Graphs (LFG or 'the Red Box') appeared on the 1987 O-level examination paper. The support materials for LFG are even more extensive than those for PPN, and have been developed to make them relevant to GCSE as well as to O-level. In a similar vein, work aimed to foster numeracy across the ability range has also adopted the model of examination driven curriculum change.

Assessing problem solving skills

PPN was developed to help children tackle more varied and more open problems than those typically found on O-level examination papers. It set out to assess the following knowledge and abilities, which are taken from the examination objectives of the JMB, which were previously inadequately assessed.

The following list is intended to provide a general indication of the knowledge and abilities which the examination will be designed to test.
1. Knowledge of mathematical notation, terminology, conventions and units. The language and notation of sets together with the ideas of a mapping and a function are basic to the syllabus.
2. The ability to understand information presented in verbal, graphical or tabular form, and to translate such information into mathematical form.
3. The ability to recognise the mathematical methods which are suitable for the solution of the problem under consideration.

4. The ability to apply mathematical methods and techniques.
5. The ability to manipulate mathematical expressions.
6. The ability to make logical deductions.
7. The ability to select and apply appropriate techniques to problems in unfamiliar or novel situations.
8. The ability to interpret mathematical results.

PPN also prepares pupils to meet assessment objectives 3.2, and 3.9 to 3.15 in the National Criteria.

Can such objectives be assessed via timed, written examinations, and scored using the current practices of Examination Boards? Questions selected for examination have not been chosen by mathematical domain, but rather in terms of the processes which can lead to their solution. Questions are generally amenable to the strategies of understanding the problem, simplifying it in some way (e.g. trying special cases), finding patterns, and generalizing the patterns found. Sample examination questions are given here; each is intended to be completed in about 20 minutes during the examination. Marking schemes described here show the proportion of credit to be assigned to various parts of the question out of a total of ten marks. One of the marking schemes is illustrated by a few pupil scripts (see Examples 1 and 2, pp. 88–95).

An activity: assessing process skills

The assessment of problem solving activities poses more problems than the assessment of mathematical technique; it is an unfamiliar activity for most people, and raises important conceptual challenges. The following activity offers the opportunity to explore some of these challenges. It is desirable to work with a colleague on this task – or even to organize a group activity for the whole department. Scripts from four pupils who tackled Skeleton Tower appear in Example 3 (pp 96–103), a grid for recording marks is shown below. Each person will need his or her own marking grid as shown in Table 6.1.

The scripts should be rank ordered and judgements entered in Table 6.1. These rankings can then form the basis for discussions with a colleague. How similar are the different people's judgements? Each person should try to justify their judgements using any descriptions which seem appropriate ('more words', 'clearer explanations', 'neater', 'free of technical errors'). Next, one should look for features of the scripts which illustrate these descriptions. Can a

Table 6.1: Record Marking Card

	Rank order	A1	A2	A3	A4	A5	A6	U	O	E	G
Ian											
Colin											
Peter											
Paul											

more detailed marking scheme be developed which reflects particular rank orderings? This process can be personally valuable; it helps make explicit the things which one values in these scripts, and offers a starting point for a discussion about them. For example, Paul has produced a very good answer, marred only by an algebraic error at the end. Should he lose marks for this, or not?

Next, a mark should be assigned to each script based on each attribute (columns A1 to A6 in Table 6.1 should be used to record scores). Discussion with a colleague will help clarify ideas; using each other's schemes will highlight areas of difficulty and should lead to improved definition of the attributes and better inter-marker reliability. Do the sums of scores on attributes produce the same rank order as the initial judgements? One may wish to change initial judgements, or attributes, or one may wish to weight attributes, so that, for example, 'clear handwriting' is worth less than 'useful generalization'.

Next try to allocate marks to each script on the process skills which the research team set out to assess: understanding; organizing; explaining; and generalization. Marks should be entered under U,O,E,G respectively, in Table 6.1. Again, results can be usefully discussed with a colleague; please review the total scores, and relate them to your original rank orderings. Our analyses are provided for comparison on pages 102–3.

The consensus arrived at, after extensive discussions, follows. Marks are coded: Pupil (Marking Scheme Score; Understanding; Organizing; Explaining; Generalizing; UOEG Score). Notice that the UOEG Score produces the same pupil ranks as the marking scheme score; halving and rounding up reconstitutes them almost exactly.

Ian	(3;	2;	3;	1;	0;	6)
Colin	(7;	5;	5;	2;	2;	14)
Peter	(6;	3;	3;	3;	0;	9)
Paul	(10;	5;	5;	5;	4;	19)

What use can be made of such scores? The most obvious benefit derives from their construction. Thinking about the things one values, and developing ways in which they can be described objectively is an essential activity for everyone involved in mathematical education. It is particularly important when slumbering assessment objectives are awakened, which relate to less tangible aspects of mathematical attainment, such as process skills. Such analyses are an essential prerequisite to investigative work in class, and indeed to any work concerned with fostering process skills. One needs clear conceptions of what one hopes to achieve in terms of improving pupil skills; intuitive judgements will not suffice.

Explanation of the skills to be acquired by pupils will form an important part of their education. It is not enough to exhort them to 'specialize', 'generalize' or 'explain better' if they are not provided with exemplars of these skills, or if the credit they receive for written work does not reflect the objectives they have been told to aim for. It may well be necesary to itemize credit on coursework using some of the headings derived here, or ones taken from the National Criteria. The virtue of such a procedure is that gaps in pupil performance become apparent. For example, a slow pupil may never get to the stages of explaining and generalizing, if teaching proceeds via 'a problem per lesson'. As a teacher, one needs to be aware of such dangers and one should allow such pupils to progress to later process stages, even if it means that slower pupils explain and generalize easier results than other children. An alternative to itemized scores is to use verbal comments only. This has the virtue that pupils' attention can be directed to areas of particular strength and weakness but runs the risk that pupils might see such work as being different to 'proper' mathematics, where progress and achievement can be measured directly. Comments on pupil work which praise the sensible use of strategies, or which offer pointers to progress, are, of course, an essential aspect of feedback for pupils during their first attempts at more open mathematics.

The language of functions and graphs

A major advantage of using mathematical languages such as graphs, tables and formulae is that a large amount of information can be compactly summarized and can be readily interpreted. In order to benefit from these advantages, one needs to practise these interpretive skills. Such skills are important across the curriculum and in life outside school where a wide range of data displays are used, which can offer guidelines for one's own decisions and whose interpretation is often critical to understanding decisions made by others.

The Language of Functions and Graphs (LFG or 'the Red Box') was developed to help children learn to interpret and use information presented in a variety of mathematical and non-mathematical forms including: verbal descriptions; graphs; tables of numbers; and algebraic expressions. It focuses on the representation of meaning in a variety of ways, and on ways of translating between these different representations. Translating between different representations does more than simply practise these skills; seeing the same concept illustrated in different representations provides an elaborated conceptual structure which is easier to work with, better integrated into other mathematical structures and subsequently easier to recall. This development of richly connected conceptual networks is an important goal of mathematical education. When knowledge is not re-formulated and the learner simply tries to store it in the form in which it is presented, new knowledge is likely to stand apart from other conceptual structures and therefore to be harder to recall when needed. Active processing of materials via such activities as discussing, translating and explaining, are all likely to lead to the development of elaborated conceptual structures.

The importance of the range of skills tackled in the Red Box is illustrated by the National Criteria which devote no less than seven criteria to this broad range of activities, namely 3.1, 3.3, 3.7, 3.10, 3.14, 3.15 and 3.16.

Mathematics offers a family of powerful languages for the description and analysis of many events. The skills of interpreting data presented in a wide variety of ways are becoming increasingly valuable as the range and number of such displays increases in the media – on television, in newspapers and magazines, and on computer screens. An important focus of the Red Box, therefore, is to focus attention on the understanding of mathematical concepts and the different ways concepts can be expressed.

All language learning involves familiarization with new symbol systems and the learning of new grammatical rules by which these symbols can be transformed. A problem with many approaches to the teaching of mathematics is that the major focus is on technical issues – for example, algebraic manipulation, point plotting and reading, filling in entries in tables – at the expense of the meaning which is to be conveyed. If an analogy is drawn with learning a foreign language, it is as if language learning proceeded by a detailed analysis of vocabulary and grammar with no attempt at sentence or paragraph comprehension. Languages are learned for a particular purpose – namely to communicate with other human beings. The same is true of mathematics; the purpose of the representations which mathematicians have invented and used is to facilitate communication between human beings and also to provide an internal language to facilitate thinking.

As in the case of the Blue Box, examination questions are provided to illustrate the range of tasks which pupils are expected to perform; the marking schemes which go with them show those aspects of task performance which are most valued. The specimen questions shown and their associated marking schemes illustrate the ways in which particular skills are to be displayed and assessed. Pupil scripts illustrate one of these marking schemes in detail (see Examples 4 and 5, pp. 104–9.)

Materials prepared for classroom use aim to develop pupils' skills in:

- interpreting graphs in practical situations;
- sketching graphs from situations presented in verbal or pictorial form;
- searching for patterns within situations, identifying functional relationships and expressing these verbally, graphically and algebraically;
- using graphs to solve problems arising from realistic situations.

The early part of the work focuses on the qualitative meaning of graphs which are set in realistic contexts. Many pupils lack understanding of the qualitative features of graphs such as the relevance of maxima and minima, discontinuities, cyclical changes and gradients. (The materials assume that technical skills such as plotting and reading points, choosing scales, drawing axes and drawing curves are already well covered in most curricula.) The second part of the teaching resource provides realistic situations for pupils to explore. Pupils are encouraged to discover patterns and functions in these data and to relate them to algebraic expressions. Throughout the work, emphasis is placed on communication; working in pairs and groups is encouraged and so too are class discussions. Detailed teaching suggestions are offered as a starting point for teachers used to working in more traditional ways in class. Of course the purpose of these teaching suggestions is to provide lesson plans which individual teachers will modify extensively as they see fit and as their experiences of working more openly develop.

Pupils are invited to reason qualitatively about the meaning of points located in a Cartesian plane; the materials set out to highlight and remediate well-known misconceptions – for example, pupil beliefs that graphs are simply pictures of the situations they represent. Pupils gain experience in translating different representations by matching verbal descriptions to sketch graphs and by sketching and interpreting graphs from pictures or situations. As work progresses more sophisticated skills of graphical interpretation are presented such as the interpretation of maxima and minima, lengths of intervals, periodicity and the interpretation of gradients. An example of a worksheet is shown in Example 6 (page 110).

Later parts of the material build on earlier skills and ask for direct translations between tables of data and sketch graphs; searching for functional relationships in situations and identifying the appropriate algebra; understanding exponential functions in the context of hypnotic drugs; and a consideration of functions with several variables (in this case, producing a model of the strength of a bridge in terms of its width, length and thickness).

The focus of the module is on language and communication; group work, therefore, plays a central part. It is essential that pupils share ideas, write about their interpretations, read materials carefully and critically and that they listen and challenge each others' ideas. Such activities practice language skills as well as equipping one to understand the language used by others. Lesson plans recommend that pupils be encouraged to work in pairs or groups; groups are encouraged to agree on sketch graphs, to write them down and to explain their methods of working and to justify solutions they produce. Teachers are encouraged to listen to pupil explanations and to stimulate pupil discussion without providing 'right' answers.

Use of the calculator is encouraged. For example, the calculator makes it possible for pupils to use realistic data concerning the rate at which different drugs wear off and to plot graphs of the decay of, say, alcohol or antidepressants in the blood stream, with time.

Numeracy

The Crowther Report (HMSO, 1959) defined numeracy as:

'the ability to deploy mathematical and other skills in tackling systematically problems of concern in every day life and in better understanding the physical, economic and social environment in which we live'.

This theme is echoed by the Cockcroft Report (HMSO, 1982):

'our concern is that those who set out to make their students "numerate" should pay attention to the wider aspects of numeracy and not be content merely to develop the skills of computation', and,

'most important of all is the need to have sufficient confidence to make effective use of whatever mathematical skill and understanding is possessed whether this be much or little'.

The JMB/SCME Numeracy Project accepted these views and set out to foster and assess pupils' ability to deploy simple mathematical and associated skills in the solution of everyday problems which pupils can reasonably be concerned with. The scheme consists of five modules, each occupying approximately four weeks of teaching time. Each module has a practical theme: modules are available on the themes of planning trips, design, running schools events, constructions using paper and card, and consumer decisions. Each module consists of a package of classroom materials which contains detailed teaching suggestions and pupil materials, together with a scheme of assessment which is designed to recognize and test skills which students have displayed during their work. The scheme has been designed for pupils of all abilities – in particular, care has been taken to ensure that materials are accessible to low attaining pupils for whom little or no public record of achievement is available at the present. A statement of achievement will be awarded to each student who performs satisfactorily. Satisfactory performance consists of demonstrating the mastery of a set of tasks which exemplify well-defined criteria. These tasks are closely related to problems which pupils will meet outside the classroom; they usually have some worthwhile practical outcome and are almost invariably based on the students' own experiences.

When technical skills are assessed, they are assessed in the context in which they will be useful in helping the students to attain some overall goal – for example, geometric skills are displayed as an integral part of producing an aesthetically pleasing board game; money management skills are assessed in the context of a trip which pupils will actually make; skills in using a stop-watch or keeping accurate records are assessed in the context of running a quiz; skills in extracting information and oral communication are assessed in the context of offering advice about which product to buy.

Pupil performance is assessed via coursework and examination. The course-work component is a record of the achievements of individual students on the tasks they have undertaken in class. The examination component requires them to recall the skills they have exhibited in class and to transfer them to other situations within the general context of the module. Two sample examination tasks are shown in Examples 7 and 8 (pp. 111–13).

Example 1:   The Climbing Game

THE CLIMBING GAME

This game is for two players.

A counter is placed on the dot labelled "start" and the players take it in turns to slide this counter up the dotted grid according to the following rules:

At each turn, the counter can only be moved to an *adjacent* dot *higher* than its current position.

Each movement can therefore only take place in one of three directions:

The first player to slide the counter to the point labelled "finish" wins the game.

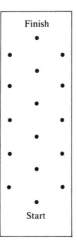

(i)   This diagram shows the start of one game, played between Sarah and Paul.

Sarah's moves are indicated by solid arrows (——►)

Paul's moves are indicated by dotted arrows (– – ►)

It is Sarah's turn. She has two possible moves.

Show that from one of these moves Sarah can ensure that she wins, but from the other Paul can ensure that he wins.

(ii)   If the game is played from the beginning and Sarah has the first move, then she can always win the game if she plays correctly.

Explain how Sarah should play in order to be sure of winning.

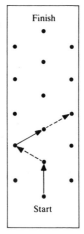

THE CLIMBING GAME . . . MARKING SCHEME

(i) **Showing an understanding of the rules of the game by systematically dealing with the various possible moves.**

1 mark for indicating that Sarah can force a win by moving to point A or for indicating that she could lose if she moves to point B.

2 marks for a correct analysis of the situation if Sarah moves to point A including the consideration of both of Paul's possible moves.

Part mark: 1 mark for an incomplete or unclear analysis.

3 marks for considering the situation if Sarah moves her counter to point B and making a correct analysis.

Part marks: 2 marks for an analysis which is complete but unclear or which is clear but omits to consider one of the two possible moves for Sarah from point A or C. 1 mark for a more partial analysis.

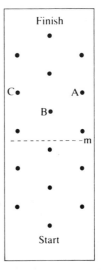

(ii) **Formulating and explaining a winning strategy for the game**

4 marks for clear, complete and correct explanation.

Part marks: 3 marks for incomplete or unclear but correct explanation.

Up to 3 marks can be given for the following:

1 mark for recognition of symmetry.

1 mark for evidence of a systematic approach.

1 mark for correctly identifying some winning and/or losing positions above line *m*.

or 2 marks for correctly identifying some winning and/or losing positions below line *m* (or above and below line *m*).

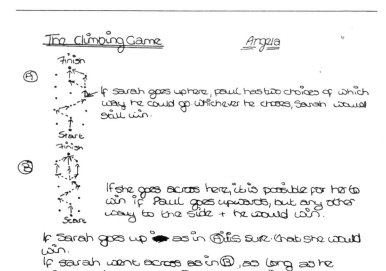

The Climbing Game   Angela

(A) Finish

If sarah goes up here, paul has two choices of which way he could go. Whichever he chooses, Sarah would still win.

Start
Finish

(B)

If she goes across here, it is possible for her to win if Paul goes upwards, but any other way to the side + he would win.

Start

If Sarah goes up as in (A) its sure that she would win.
If sarah went across as in (B), as long as he didn't go upwards, Paul would win.

The climbing game   Daren

FINISH

• B

• C

• A

START

This is the start of the game between Sarah and Paul. Sarahs moves are indicated by the solid lines, and Pauls moves are indicated by the dotted arrows. From this position Sarah can ensure a win or ensure that Paul wins. If she moves to point B, she will win, because no matter where paul then moves, it will leave Sarah with just one move to make to the finish. If she moves to point c, she will ensure herself of defeat because she will put paul in the winning position.

The following examples exhibit various features of the marking scheme.

Part (i) Marking Incomplete Analyses

Both Angela and Darren gain 3 marks (out of a possible 3) for correctly analysing the situation if Sarah moves vertically upwards. In the case when Sarah moves diagonally upwards both candidates produced incomplete analyses. However Angela's analysis is only lacking in the consideration of the case illustrated below:–

Finish

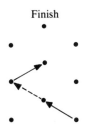

Her analysis would be awarded 2 marks out of the possible 3 marks.

Darren's analysis does not explain why Sarah's move to the point Darren labels "C" puts Paul in a winning position. This is less complete than Angela's analysis and is awarded 1 mark out of the possible 3 marks.

Steven

I've shown both routes
that Paul can take from
Sarah's moves and he can't
win.

The dark ones are Sarah
The dotted ones are Paul
This way Sarah can't lose
Sarah can also win on the
otherside as well.

Finish   Michael

winning
positions to move
onto

Whichever move he
makes, take the counter
to the point "X".

2) If you starts first then you should take the line
left or right to the next point. Wherever he moves, take
the line to the cross on the diagram. He has a choice
of 3 moves, Whichever one it is, take the line to the
spot marked O. From here he will play the counter to a
point adjacent to the Finish and you have won!

Part (ii) Marking Explanations

Explanations can be given using diagrams or verbal descriptions, or a combination of the two.

Steven's explanation is almost entirely diagrammatic. His diagram shows the moves that Sarah must make and two alternative moves that Paul can make at each stage. The cases which are not covered by the diagram follow from the symmetry of the situation and this is implied by Steven's statement: "Sarah can also win on the other side as well!"

By contrast Michael's explanation is more verbal. Whereas Steven considers sequences of moves from start to finish, Michael identifies winning positions, which he clearly defines as positions he moves *onto*.

(Some other candidates may use an alternative definition of "winning positions" as points *from* which you can win if it is your turn to move.)

Both Steven and Michael are awarded the full 4 marks for their explanations.

Example 2:   Stepping Stones

STEPPING STONES

A ring of "stepping stones" has 14 stones in it, as shown in the diagram.

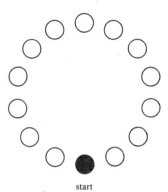

start

A girl hops round the ring, stopping to change feet every time she has made 3 hops. She notices that when she has been round the ring three times, she has stopped to change feet on each one of the 14 stones.

(i)   The girl now hops round the ring, stopping to change feet every time she has made 4 hops. Explain why in this case she will not stop on each one of the 14 stones no matter how long she continues hopping round the ring.

(ii) The girl stops to change feet every time she has made n hops. For which values of n will she stop on each one of the 14 stones to change feet?

(iii) Find a general rule for the values of n when the ring contains more (or less) than 14 stones.

STEPPING STONES . . . MARKING SCHEME

(i) **Showing an understanding of the problem through explaining a simple case.**

3 marks for a clear, correct and complete explanation.

Part marks: Give 2 marks for an incomplete but otherwise clear and correct explanation.

In other cases 1 or 2 marks may be gained by mentioning one or two of the following:

    (a) Evenness or common factor 2;

    (b) After going twice round, the girl returns to the starting stone;

    (c) The girl stops on 7 of the 14 stones (or every other stone).

(ii) **Considering other cases and organising the information.**

4 marks for $n=3, 5, 9, 11, 13$ (condone the omission of 1 and values of n greater than 14).

Part marks: Give 3 marks if the solution contains one error (e.g. includes 2 or omits 11) but $n=7$ is clearly rejected.

Give 2 marks for at least three correct values of n with $n=7$ clearly rejected.

Give 1 mark for one correct value of n (other than $n=1$, $n=3$) or a correct general statement such as "n must be an odd number".

(iii) **Generalising by considering further cases and formulating a rule.**

1 mark for considering case(s) with more (or less) than 14 stones.

2 marks for a general rule which is clear, correct and complete.

Part mark: Give 1 mark for a general rule which is apparently correct but not very clear.

Example 3:   Skeleton Tower

SKELETON TOWER

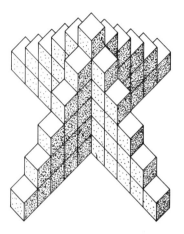

(i)   How many cubes are needed to build this tower?

(ii) How many cubes are needed to build a tower like this, but 12 cubes high?

(iii) Explain how you worked out your answer to part (ii).

(iv) How would you calculate the number of cubes needed for a tower *n* cubes high?

IAN

Skeleton Tower

1) ~~20 + 15 + ...~~ = ~~50 cubes~~. 20 + 16 + 12 + 8 + 4 + 1 = 61

2) ~~1 + 4 + 6 + 20~~ 1 + 4 + 8 + 12 + 16 + 20 + 24 + 28 + 32 + 36 + 40 + 44 + 48
= 313 cubes.

35 113 135 171 211 255 283·5

3) In question 2 there is a pattern which goes up in 4,s eg 1st level = 1, 2nd = 4, 3rd = 8 and so on, so I just did what until I came to the height of 12 cubes.

4) cubes = ~~height of cubes~~ 1 layer × 4 + on
A quarter of the ~~tower~~ bottom   20 mins
layer is 5 in Q1, multiply 5 × 4, and you have the number of cubes in the bottom layer.

COLIN

Skeleton Tower:

The amount of cubes needed to build the tower are 66

Height (H)	amount of cubes (c)	width of base (w)	amount of steps (s)
6 7	66	11	5
7 8	~~78~~ 91	13	6
8 9	~~2~~120	15	7
9 10	153	17	8
10 11	190	19	9
11 12	221	21	10
12	256	23	11

Amount of steps = height minus one
Width of base = amount of steps multiplied by two add one
Amount of cubes = height multiplied by width of base

So a tower of height 12 would need 256 cubes to be
constructed out of.

$$w = 2s + 1 \qquad s = \frac{c}{w} - 1$$
$$c = H \times w \qquad w = \frac{c}{H} \qquad H = \frac{c}{w}$$
$$s = H - 1 \qquad H = s + 1$$

As the height increases by one the width goes up by two

PETER

(1) $15 \times 4 = 60 + 6 = 66$ Cubes are needed to build this tower.

(2)
$$4 \times 6 = 24$$
$$4 \times 7 = 28$$
$$4 \times 8 = 32$$
$$4 \times 9 = 36$$
$$4 \times 10 = 40$$
$$4 \times 11 = 44$$
$$+ \quad + \quad 6$$
$$\overline{210}$$

210 cubes are needed to make a tower 12 cubes high.

3) I counted the number of cubes down one side on the top edge which came to 5 Excluding the centre one. Adding on each time to 5 and the multiplying by 4 each time then adding the 6 centre ones I came to the answer of 210 cubes.

PAUL

SKELETON TOWER.

The tower has 5 stories each going upwards downwards. in numerical order ie 1.2.3.4.5. the formular for numerical numbers in order or triangular numbers is

$$\frac{x^2 + x}{2}$$

The tower could be made up of two triangles each 11 blocks on the bottom side and ascend 11.9.7.5.3.1. The middle 5 blocks of one triangle are replaced by the other triangle which whose middle 5 blocks has been removed. An overhead view of the triangles is in the shape of a cross.

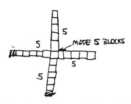

5
5
MIDDLE 5 BLOCKS
5
5

1. For each part of the tower tower ie the five blocked base, use the formula for triangular numbers.

$$\frac{x^2 + x}{2} = \frac{5^2 + 5}{2} = \frac{30}{2} = 15$$

now multiply this by 4 (the four parts)

$$15 \times 4 = 60$$

Now add 6 (the middle six blocks)

$$60 + 6 = 66 \text{ BLOCKS}.$$

2 & 3 To build a tower 12 cubes high

Take away the middle twelve blocks so you are left with for eleven blocked

continued

PAUL (continued)

triangles then use the formula of triangular numbers for one part of the tower.

$$\therefore \frac{x^2+x}{2} = \frac{11^2+11}{2} = \frac{132}{2} = 66$$

Now I multiply this number by 4.

$$66 \times 4 = 264$$

Now add twelve =

$$264 + 12 = 276 \ blocks$$

4. For a tower n cubes high:

Take away the middle n blocks; you are left with 4 blocks of $n-1$ high. Then use the following equation

$$\frac{x^2+x}{2} = \frac{(n-1)^2+(n-1)}{2} \ \neq =$$

Now multiply this number by 4.

$$\frac{(4n-1)^2+(4n-1)}{2}$$

Then add n to the total.

$$\frac{(4n-1)^2+(4n-1)}{2} + n = \text{NUMBER OF BLOCKS NEEDED TO MAKE A SKELETON TOWER OF } n \text{ BLOCKS HIGH.}$$

SKELETON TOWER . . . MARKING SCHEME

(i) **Showing an understanding of the problem by dealing correctly with a simple case.**

Answer: 66

2 marks for a correct answer (with or without working).

Part mark: Give 1 mark if a correct method is used but there is an arithmetical error.

(ii) **Showing a systematic attack in the extension to a more difficult case.**

Answer: 276

4 marks if a correct method is used and the correct answer is obtained.

Part marks: Give 3 marks if a correct method is used but the work contains an arithmetical error or shows a misunderstanding (e.g. 13 cubes in the centre column).

Give 2 marks if a correct method is used but the work contains two arithmetical errors/misunderstandings.

Give 1 mark if the candidate has made some progress but the work contains more than two arithmetical errors/misunderstandings.

(iii) **Describing the methods used.**

2 marks for a correct, clear, complete description of what has been done providing more than one step is involved.

Part mark: Give 1 mark if the description is incomplete or unclear but apparently correct.

(iv) **Formulating a general rule verbally or algebraically.**

2 marks for a correct, clear, complete description of method.

Accept "number of cubes$=n(2n-1)$" or equivalent for 2 marks. Ignore any errors in algebra if the description is otherwise correct, clear and complete.

Part mark: Give 1 mark if the description is incomplete or unclear but shows that the candidate has some idea how to obtain the result for any given value of n.

NOTES ON MARKED SCRIPTS

Ian   Ian has misunderstood the question and assumed the tower to have a hollow middle.

In part (i) his answer is therefore wrong and he gets no marks.

In part (ii) he has made two errors: he assumed the tower has a hollow middle and has 13 layers. He was therefore given 2 marks out of 4.

In part (iii), his explanation of his calculation is not complete and so he scores 1 mark out of 2.

In part (iv) his answer is not correct and scores no marks.

Colin   In part (ii) Colin has made two errors in multiplication for $h=11$ and $h=12$. Since each answer has been worked out independently using $c=h \times w$ only the error in $h=12$ need be penalised. So Colin scores 3 marks out of 4.

In part (iii) he scored both marks for a clear, complete and correct explanation of his method.

In part (iv) the three formulae on the left hand side are correct and sufficient to solve the problem, although they are not organised systematically. He was therefore awarded 1 mark out of 2.

Peter   In part (ii) there is some doubt as to how Peter has worked out his answer. It may be that he has attempted to build onto the original tower and calculated the number of extra cubes needed but has forgotten to add on the 66. We are giving him the benefit of the doubt by taking this view although this may mean a slightly inflated mark. He was awarded 3 marks out of 4 for part (ii).

In part (iii) his explanation of his method is not very clear and he was awarded 1 mark out of 2.

Paul   Paul's answer is of a very high standard. He was awarded 10 marks out of 10 despite the algebraic error in the last part.

Example 4: Camping

CAMPING

On their arrival at a campsite, a group of campers are given a piece of string 50 metres long and four flag poles with which they have to mark out a rectangular boundary for their tent.

They decide to pitch their tent next to a river as shown below. This means that the string has to be used for only three sides of the boundary.

(i) If they decide to make the width of the boundary 20 metres, what will the length of the boundary be?

(ii) Describe in words, as fully as possible, how the length of the boundary changes as the width increases through all possible values. (Consider both small and large values of the width.)

(iii) Find the area enclosed by the boundary for a width of 20 metres and for some other different widths.

(iv) Draw a *sketch* graph to show how the area enclosed changes as the width of the boundary increases through all possible values. (Consider both small and large values of the width.)

The campers are interested in finding out what the length and the width of the boundary should be to obtain the greatest possible area.

(v) Describe, in words, a method by which you could find this length and width.

(vi) Use the method you have described in part (v) to find this length and width.

CAMPING...MARKING SCHEME

(i) and (ii) Describing a functional relationship using words

(i)   *1 mark*   for length = 10m.

(ii)   *3 marks*   for 'As the width increases from 0 to 25m, the length decreases linearly (uniformly) from 50m to 0m'.

                         or for 'As the width increases, the length decreases at twice the rate'.

                         Part marks: Give 2 marks for 'As the width increases the length decreases linearly (uniformly)'

                         or 2 marks for 'As the width increases from 0m to 25m, the length decreases from 50m to 0m'

                         or 1 mark for 'As the width increases, the length decreases'.

(iii) and (iv) Translating information into a mathematical representation.

(iii)   *1 mark*   for area = 200m^2.

         2 marks   for finding correct areas for three other widths.

                         Part mark: 1 mark for finding correct areas for two other widths.

(iv)   *2 marks*   for a sketch graph which shows a continuous curve with a single maximum point.

                         Part mark: Give 1 mark for a sketch graph which is wholly or partly straight or consists of discrete points, but shows that the area increases and then decreases.

(v) Describing the method to be used in solving a problem.

         3 marks   for a clear and complete description of how to find both dimensions.

                         Part mark: Give 2 marks for a clear and complete description of how to find only one of the dimensions.

                         Give 1 mark if the explanation is not clear but apparently correct.

(vi) Using mathematical representations to solve a problem.

         2 marks   for 'width = 12.5m for maximum area'.

                         Part mark: Give 1 mark for a width given in the interval 12m < width < 13m.

                         or 1 mark for 'width could be 12m or 13m'.

         1 mark   for 'length = 25m for maximum area'.

                         (follow through an incorrect width in the interval 12m ⩽ width ⩽ 13m).

A total of 15 marks are available for this question.

Example 5:   The Hurdles Race

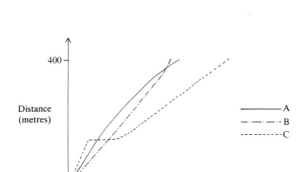

THE HURDLES RACE

The rough sketch graph shown above describes what happens when 3 athletes A, B and C enter a 400 metres hurdles race.

Imagine that you are the race commentator. Describe what is happening as carefully as you can. You do not need to measure anything accurately.

THE HURDLES RACE...MARKING SCHEME

Interpreting a mathematical representation using words.

1 mark	for 'C takes the lead'
1 mark	for 'C stops running'
1 mark	for 'B overtakes A'
1 mark	for 'B wins'
2 marks	for any four of the following:

  A and B pass C
  C starts running again
  C runs at a slower pace
  A slows down (or B speeds up)
  A finishes 2nd (or C finishes last)

  Part mark: 1 mark if any two (or three) of the above points are mentioned.

2 marks   for a lively commentary which mentions hurdles.

  Part mark: 1 mark for a lively commentary which does not mention hurdles, or for a 'report' which mentions hurdles.

A total of 8 marks are available for this question.

Martin

And they were off. C increased speed very rapidly for the first 150 m and covered a big distance in a very short time. B took it calmly and paced himself to his limits he went reasonably fast and A went faster than B but slower than C at the start, but then C stopped for a rest and carried on slowly coming in last A went faster and kept going, but was overtaken by B who beat A and came first, B won, A was second, and C was third.

Stephen

Here at the start off the race the three athletes are ready to start. There off. Athlete C takes an early lead, Athlete A is close in second and athlete B is in the rear after a bad start. They're approaching the 100m mark. It's still C leading from A and B is catching up Oh no, C as fall. He's getting up and chasing A and B. At half way A has a small lead again but B is gradually catching him and it looks like C hasn't much chance of winning. There now in the final 100m A and B are neck and neck, C has just passed halfway. Athlete A crosses the line first be is only just behind him. C is about 100m out. I think C might have won if he didn't fall.

Wendy

<u>Athlete A</u> came 2nd - He started off fairly fast and got slightly slower during the race.

<u>Athlete B</u> came 1st - He started off at a steady rate and picked up speed all the way through the race.

<u>Athlete C</u> came 3rd - He started off going fast, then he fell over and didn't run for a few seconds, then he started running again, gradually getting slower and slower.

Marking the descriptions

Martin has mentioned all of the first 4 factors and also 3 of the additional ones. For this he scored 5 marks. Martin's commentary reads more like a report than a commentary, and since he does not mention the hurdles, he was not awarded any "commentary" marks. Therefore, Martin obtained a total of 5 marks out of the possible 8.

Stephen has only mentioned 2 of the first 4 factors and 2 of the additional ones, thus scoring 3 marks. However, Stephen's commentary is lively and interesting although he has ignored the fact that it is a hurdles race. He was awarded one "commentary" mark, making a total of 4 out of the possible 8.

Wendy has also mentioned 2 of the first 4 points, as well as 3 of the additional ones. She was awarded 3 marks for these. Wendy does not, however, obtain any "commentary" marks, since she has described each athlete's run separately, rather than giving a commentary on the race as a whole.

Example 6: Sketching graphs from pictures

A4 SKETCHING GRAPHS FROM PICTURES

Motor Racing

How do you think the speed of a racing car will vary as it travels on the *second lap* around each of the three circuits drawn below? (S = starting point)

Circuit 1   Circuit 2   Circuit 3

Explain your answer in each case both in words and with a sketch graph. State clearly any assumptions that you make.

Speed ↑

→ Distance along track

Compare your graphs with those produced by your neighbours. Try to produce three graphs which you all agree are correct.

1

Look again at the graph you drew for the third circuit. In order to discover how good your sketch is, answer the following questions looking *only* at your sketch graph. When you have done this, check your answer by looking back at the picture of the circuit. If you find any mistakes *redraw* your sketch graph.

— Is the car on the first or second lap?

— How many bends are there on the circuit?

— Which bend is the most dangerous?

— Which "straight" portion of the circuit is the longest? Which is the shortest?

— Does the car begin the third lap with the same speed as it began the second? Should it?

Now invent a racing circuit of your own with, at most, four bends.

Sketch a graph *on a separate sheet of paper* to show how the speed of a car will vary as it goes around your circuit.

Pass *only* your graph to your neighbour.

Can she reconstruct the shape of the original racing circuit?

2

The Big Wheel

The Big Wheel in the diagram turns round once every 20 seconds. On the same pair of axes, sketch two graphs to show how both the height of car A and the height of car B will vary during a minute.

Describe how your graphs will change if the wheel turns more quickly.

Orbits

Each of the diagrams below shows a spacecraft orbiting a planet at a constant speed.

Sketch two graphs to show how the distance of the spacecraft from the planet will vary with time.

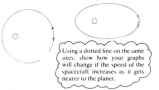

Using a dotted line on the same axes, show how your graphs will change if the speed of the spacecraft increases as it gets nearer to the planet.

Now invent your own orbits and sketch their graphs, *on a separate sheet of paper*. Give *only* your graphs to your neighbour. Can she reconstruct the orbits from the graphs alone?

4

The graph below shows how the speed of a racing car varies during the second lap of a race.

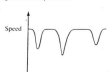

Speed ↑

Distance along the track

Which of these circuits was it going round?

Discuss this problem with your neighbours.
Write down your reasons each time you reject a circuit.

3

Example 7: Build a Pyramid

<u>Design a Board Game</u> module examination - an Extension Level specimen paper

Build a Pyramid

This is a game for 2 players

Aim

The first player to build a pyramid with 15 counters, wins the game.

Equipment

One board for each player
15 counters for each player
2 dice, one black and one white.

  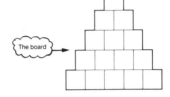

Preparation

Each player fills her board with numbers. A number from the set {1, 2, 3, 4, 5} must be written in each square. A player can choose to place some or all of these numbers in any position. For example, here are three possible ways:

Rules

- Decide which player will be 'BLACK' and which will be 'WHITE'.

- Throw the two dice.

- If the number on the black dice is greater than the number on the white dice, then BLACK calculates the *difference* between the two numbers on the dice and covers any correspondingly numbered square on her board with a counter.

- Similarly, if the number on the white dice is greater than the number on the black dice, then WHITE calculates the difference and covers a corresponding square on her board.

- If both numbers on the dice are equal, neither player covers a number.

- The first player to cover all 15 squares and complete the pyramid wins the game.

Build a Pyramid

Suppose that the two boards are filled in like this:

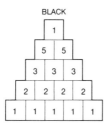
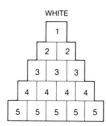

1. The first four throws of the dice are:

 ; ; ;

   On copies of the boards, show clearly which numbers have been covered.

2. Which player do you think is most likely to win?

   (If you think that both players are equally likely to win, write 'You can't tell').

   Give a reason to support your answer.

3. Now suppose that *you* were playing the game.

   (a) Show how *you* would number *your* board to give the best chance of winning.

   (b) Explain *why* you think this would give you the best chance of winning.

4. Suppose that the game is to be adapted for 3 players using 3 dice and 3 boards. Describe how you would adapt the rules, so that the game will still work.

Example 8: Star

Star

The diagram below shows a small board design for playing a game called 'Star'.

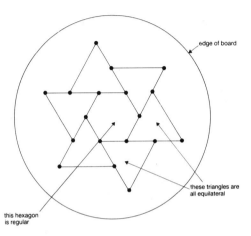

edge of board

these triangles are
all equilateral

this hexagon
is regular

The game will be played with circular counters, 2 cm in diameter.

The counters will be placed on the 18 black blobs (marked ●) on the board.

The board must be large enough so that when the counters are placed on adjacent 'blobs', there is a 1 cm gap between them, and no counter is ever less than 1 cm from the edge of the board.

This distance must be
1 cm

Draw an accurate board which will satisfy these conditions.

7 Investigations

One of the main purposes of investigational work is to foster pupil autonomy in their mathematical activities. If pupils are to treat mathematics as a recreational topic from which they can derive pleasure outside the classroom, investigational work can provide a good starting point. From a simple mathematical seed, pupils are expected to carry out some investigation of their own choosing and to follow their findings towards more general results and conclusions. Such activities require open-ended styles of teaching and learning. Assessing such activities requires a good deal of skill.

The conduct of investigations requires pupils to organize their work for themselves, to engage in mathematical activities such as drawing diagrams, devising their own notations, explaining their results and describing their methods of working. Investigations can provide sources of evidence about many of the activities in the National Criteria which can be difficult to obtain in other ways. Process skills such as generalizing, conjecturing, working systematically, generating hypotheses and testing them and devising mathematical notations, can be an integral part of investigational work and can provide evidence that pupils have acquired some of these skills.

Although investigational work sounds as if it poses hard mathematical challenges, many tasks are suitable for investigation by young pupils and by pupils of lower attainment. Nevertheless, fostering investigations in class is by no means a simple matter. Handling pupil problems and questions can be difficult. Offering detailed guidance about how to proceed, and suggesting likely fertile avenues removes important potential learning situations from pupils, although it might appear to lead to rapid progress compared to more painful methods of pupil exploration, partial success, modification, followed by more partial success. Investigational work often rewards mastery of mathematical technique with success, and punishes technical inaccuracies heavily – since it is almost impossible to spot patterns and relationships when these patterns contain technical errors. Answering pupil queries about technical matters therefore requires fine judgement. Since the purpose of the activity is rarely to practise technical skills, error detection, and perhaps correction, by the teacher and the provision of technical advice can be worthwhile. However, there is a danger that if the teacher provides too much technical support, pupils will not see the need to do it for themselves.

Group work is often an appropriate setting for investigational work, in part because of the checking which pupils can do for each other. Activities such as explanation, articulation of hypotheses and testing conjectures follow naturally when pupils are set to work in pairs. So too do monitoring remarks where pupils will readily ask each other, 'why should we do that now?', 'what are we really trying to do?'.

Investigative work is not defined by content (for example, Pick's Theorem, Diagonals of a Rectangle, Squares on a Chessboard, and other old favourites) rather, it refers to a particular approach to mathematics. The starting point of an investigation is somewhat irrelevant; the critical feature of investigative work is the mathematical development that takes place. To illustrate this assertion a very dull starting point has been chosen quite deliberately in the example which follows. (The intended message is that almost any piece of mathematics can form the seed for an investigation, not that dullness is unimportant!)

Investigations and associative memory

Pupils who are unfamiliar with investigative work are often surprised at how much of the mathematics they know can be brought to bear on the investigation in hand. It is worth encouraging a phase of 'free association' when pupils first tackle investigations – pupils can be invited to keep a list of everything they think of – both when they consider the problem, and as they progress. This list should be reviewed regularly as a source of ideas for new developments, or as a source of ideas for linking together themes already explored. As an example of the rich source of material in memory, please spend five minutes exploring this (somewhat unpromising) seed. Simply write down your mental associations to the problem, and sketch out some lines of investigation which might be adopted.

Explore the following:
$1 + 2 =$
A number of distinct approaches can be taken.

Series

$1+2$ is the start of the series:
$1+2+3+...$

This series occurs quite often in work on number investigations, and children tackle the problem in an interesting variety of ways. For example:

(a)   Forward and backward sums:
    sum $= 1 + 2 \quad + 3 \quad + ... \quad n{-}2 + n{-}1 + n$
    sum $= n + n{-}1 + n{-}2 + ... \quad 3 \quad + 2 \quad + 1$
    So $2 \times$ sum $= n$ lots of $n{+}1$
    or, sum $= \dfrac{n(n+1)}{2}$

(b)   An interesting geometric version is shown in Figure 7.1.

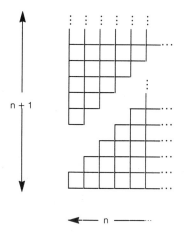

Figure 7.1: A geometric approach

(c)   More algebraic methods
    If n is even:
    $1+2+3+...n = (1+n) + (2+n-1) + ...(\frac{n}{2}+(\frac{n}{2}+1))$,
    i.e. $\frac{n}{2}$ terms, each of $(n+1)$.
    If n is odd, the same sum can be done for $(n-1)$, add back the n, and juggle the algebra.
    $\dfrac{(n-1)n}{2} + n = \dfrac{n(n+1)}{2}$

(d)   Proof by induction is often illustrated using the sum of this series.

Each of the methods (a) to (d) and their intimate associations are available in teachers' memories and are potential sources of inspiration when they do investigative work.

Consecutive sums

One and two are consecutive whole numbers. A related problem was included in Problems with Patterns and Numbers.

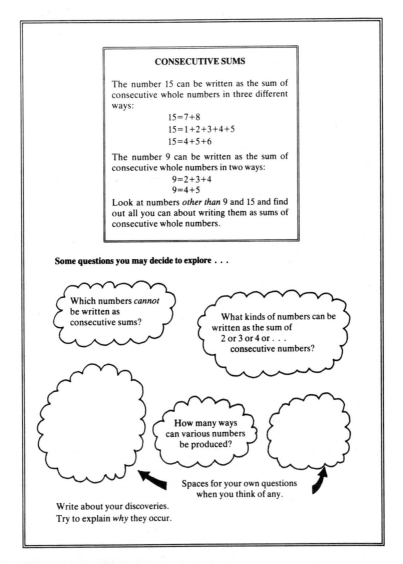

CONSECUTIVE SUMS

The number 15 can be written as the sum of consecutive whole numbers in three different ways:

$$15=7+8$$
$$15=1+2+3+4+5$$
$$15=4+5+6$$

The number 9 can be written as the sum of consecutive whole numbers in two ways:

$$9=2+3+4$$
$$9=4+5$$

Look at numbers *other than* 9 and 15 and find out all you can about writing them as sums of consecutive whole numbers.

Some questions you may decide to explore . . .

Which numbers *cannot* be written as consecutive sums?

What kinds of numbers can be written as the sum of 2 or 3 or 4 or . . . consecutive numbers?

How many ways can various numbers be produced?

Spaces for your own questions when you think of any.

Write about your discoveries.
Try to explain *why* they occur.

Example 9: Consecutive sums

A number of conjectures can be made readily by pupils such as:

> its easy to make odd numbers like this
> you can't always do it for even numbers, but sometimes you
> can...
> big numbers don't necessarily have more ways to do it than
> smaller ones.

To get a reasonable account of questions such as:

> Which numbers cannot be written as consecutive sums?
> How many different ways can various numbers be produced?

one needs a story which involves prime numbers, powers, a proof by construction and a proof by contradiction (or rather, I did, when I explored it).

These proofs and this exploration can all be reconstructed and brought to the centre of attention by the simple starting point '1 + 2 = ...'.

This range of approaches derived directly from my associative memory and the links between them are rather tenuous. No doubt your own associations and ideas for investigations were at least as rich and varied as mine. When solving unfamiliar problems these links can be used to offer starting points, to suggest representations and to suggest fruitful directions for exploration. As mathematical knowledge develops, so too does the richness of the memory associations which can be called upon to help explore new situations.

How can these associations be used?

Pupils should be encouraged to write down both their initial associations and everything that springs to mind during an investigation. Reviewing this list during the course of investigation, or when stuck, can suggest new linkages and new directions for exploration. Just as importantly, it can foster the development of more integrated mathematical structures, by drawing attention to the similarities between different structures in algebra, geometry and number work, for example.

A more methodical approach to investigation and exploration is to begin by systematically identifying features of the problem and their associations. These can be explored in their own right. For example, notice that:

$1+2=2+1.$

For which operations is this true $(+, -, \div, \times)$? (This can lead off into questions involving commutativity and the use of apparatus for illustrative purposes.) But what happens if the numbers change?

$10+20=30$

So why doesn't $17+27=37$? 'One seven plus two sevens is three sevens, isn't it miss?' (This can lead off into practice of arithmetic; conceptions of place value; pupil conceptions and misconceptions in general.) What happens if numbers are added on?

$1+2+3+\ldots=$

(This leads to series and sums of series.) What happens if the starting point is changed?

$7+8=15$
or $2+3=5$

(This leads to consecutive sums and all their associations.) What happens if the addition continues?

$1+2=3; \quad 2+3=5; \quad 3+5=8; \quad 5+8=13\ldots$

(This leads to an exploration of *Fibonacci* series.) How many ways are there to produce the same number?

$1+2=1{\cdot}5+1{\cdot}5=\ldots$

(This can lead into graphical work and conceptions of infinity.)

So, a combination of one's associations, and a systematic analysis of the features of a problem can provide a rich source of ideas for investigative work and can show the interconnected nature of mathematical knowledge.

Managing investigations in class

Investigative mathematics is not about using a particular set of problems, but involves engaging in a particular style of interaction with pupils, and facilitating a wide range of pupil approaches to exploring particular families of mathematical ideas.

Experience in managing problem-solving in class is an essential prerequisite to the management of investigational work. Starting points for stimulating problem-solving activities are available in the 'Blue Box'; there is little point in reproducing them here. Those materials begin by setting pupils well-defined tasks which show some pay-off from the use of strategies (such as: try simple cases; find a helpful diagram; organize systematically; spot patterns; explain why a rule works) which they practise while solving problems. From this rather 'closed' beginning, pupil autonomy increases until pupils face unstructured problems which they tackle in any way they choose – hopefully deploying general strategies and monitoring their performance as they proceed. As well as a reduction in the written help available to pupils, the hints given to pupils by teachers change as pupils learn to direct their efforts for themselves. If pupils are to face open mathematical challenges, they must learn how to decide what to do and when to do it. If someone always tells them what to do, they won't learn these skills. A hierarchy of help is offered which is rather like a calorie controlled diet; some remarks are nutritious and wholesome; others give immediate pleasure but are bad for long-term health. This is relevant to the conduct of investigations, too. Some highlights are listed below.

Use freely any hints that make children think about the way they are tackling the problem:

> what are you trying to do;
> why are we doing this;
> what will we do when we get this result;
> well, what do you think?

Use sparingly, particularly later on, hints about which strategies they should use:

> how can we organize this;
> can you see any pattern;
> what examples should you choose;
> have you checked if that works?

Avoid any hint reterring to the particular problem:

> do you recognize square numbers;
> explore it like this;
> why don't you try using 3 counters?

These and similar remarks can be useful when helping pupils to carry out investigations. In addition, all the remarks made later about the management and assessment of group work and class discussion are relevant to the conduct of investigations.

Assessing investigations

Assessment of the outcome from investigative work – that is to say, the mathematical discoveries made and the way they are presented by the pupil – requires a similar development process to the one followed in assessing process skills, described in an earlier chapter. This can be summarized briefly, as follows:

One should begin with a few scripts – say five or six – and a colleague willing to share the experience.

Scripts are put into rank order from best to worst and notes are made about features which are particularly valued (or disliked).

Then the ordering of the scripts is discussed, using the list of desirable features and exemplars of each. The National Criteria provide a useful source of ideas about desirable features. For example: clarity of presentation; quality of reasoning, generalization, and proof; exploration of patterns and relationships; quality of creative and imaginative mathematics; systematic investigation (tables, simple cases...); linkage across different branches of mathematics; and quality of mathematical language.

A table can be constructed like Table 6.1 whose rows form the names of pupil authors of the scripts, and whose columns are labelled with desirable attributes. Each script is then marked on each attribute.

Tables can then be compared with those produced by colleagues. Do atomistic judgements give essentially the same results as initial, holistic, judgements?

The activity can be repeated as often as seems desirable – initial rank ordering, the attributes chosen, or the marks given to each script on each attribute can each be revised.

The purpose of the whole activity is to help the development of a system of judgement that individual teachers and the whole department feel happy with; it is not an exercise in defending initial impressions.

The conduct and assessment of investigations are intimately linked. Asking a pupil to describe approaches, hypotheses, results and next lines of attack is an excellent opportunity to assess and improve skills in oral mathematics, as well as to monitor and foster investigative skills. Teachers can be placed in an unusual position when listening to a pupil's account of an investigation. Often, the pupil will know more about this particular mathematical topic than the teacher, and it is important for the listener to adopt the role of 'fellow pupil' from the outset (even if a pupil is treading well-worn paths, this role has considerable advantages for the purpose of discussion). Pupils should be asked to explain their progress clearly (e.g. to review their activities, including blind alleys and getting stuck in technical 'busy work'). Such reflection on the way mental effort has been spent is likely to have benefits for future occasions. Asking for a description of findings brings one face to face with pupils as mathematicians! One should try to speak less and to listen more; to ask for explanations of things that are not clear ('can you say that in a simpler way' is better than 'garbled – try again'). Counter examples should be offered rather than contradictions ('what would your theory produce for four counters? Will you check it for me?' is better than 'that can't be right – it doesn't work for four counters'). Questions about presentation should be raised before pupils begin to write up their work.

Pupils who are unfamiliar with investigative work need to know the ground rules of the new game, and need exemplars of good investigative work, and less good investigative work. Explicit descriptions of the marking scheme will be worthwhile; itemized scores on pupil work are worthy of consideration, but will, of course, be supplemented by detailed written comments. Classroom display of investigations can also provide examples of the sort of written work that pupils should aspire to.

8 Assessing Groupwork

Groupwork is one of Cockcroft's 'missing activities' which should become an essential part of mathematical learning. Nevertheless, exhortations are of little use unless they are associated with ideas for how to get things going, how to assess progress, and how to improve the quality of groupwork as work progresses. This chapter will attempt to offer guidance on each of these themes.

Groupwork has to be *about* something; a variety of tasks which were described earlier as illustrations of work on problem solving, investigational work, graphical interpretation and practical work provide appropriate starting points. The most obvious feature of groupwork is that pupils talk together – this can be desultory off-task chat, but it is to be hoped that a rare flower will blossom: on-task oral mathematics.

Why work in groups?

Groupwork can involve problems of class management, increased noise, (which may be unpopular with colleagues in adjacent classrooms) and perhaps rowdiness; discussions which degenerate into social conversation; a dominant pupil who awes others into quiescence; pupils who become passengers, involuntarily, or voluntarily; reduced pupil self-image if ideas are not valued by other group members, or if the tone of groupwork is highly critical, or if other people are felt to be far better at the activity than they are; and frenetic teaching, where one is driven to dash around from group to group, in order to bolster motivation, and to check that groupwork is productive.

So why should pupils be asked to work in groups? Groupwork is inherently valuable outside classrooms; few people work alone on problems. If pupils are to acquire skills in class which are useful outside, some experience of groupwork where they can share expertise is essential. Groupwork can be more effective than individual work; a number of studies have shown that the performance of a group facing items from a set of problems is superior to the performance of the most able group member, faced with items from the same set.

Pupils can also practice social skills involved in the conduct of discussions, negotiation, and a range of personal skills (taking turns, eliciting and respecting and building upon the views of others) as well as practising oral mathematical skills. Groupwork helps pupils to talk about planning skills in a natural way. Challenges such as 'why are we doing this?', 'suppose we do decide to do it your way, what happens after we've counted up all those blocks?'; insights like 'we need to check each other's work' or 'this is crazy – we're all doing different things and aren't sharing the results', occur naturally, and draw pupils' attention to the need to plan, to review, to be systematic and to check regularly when doing mathematics.

Talking to pupils about mathematical processes is almost impossible unless the discussion is embedded in some context. Groupwork provides an excellent context because planning remarks occur naturally and are seen by pupils to be important to the overall success of the activity. Pupils often check each other's work, and detect trivial errors in computation. Had these remained undetected, they would almost certainly have doomed subsequent attempts to spot number patterns which form the basis for a generalization of the patterns detected. So groupwork can help more pupils to progress to later stages of problem solving (spotting relationships, generalizing results) than they might have got to, working individually. Pupils are responsible for the intellectual management of tasks, so groupwork can foster autonomy. Pupils can successfully tackle harder problems in groups than they could manage on their own. Groupwork allows teachers to observe individual patterns of working, and subsequently scope to coach individuals and groups in order to remediate gaps (e.g., in process skills such as 'being systematic' or 'trying simple cases') and to praise strengths (quality of discussion, presentation of results, allocation of tasks between group members, regular monitoring of progress to avoid 'busy work' and dead ends).

Some valuable activities can only be done collaboratively. Games, for example, usually require a good deal of logical analysis, forward thinking, and planning for different contingencies ('if she does that, then I'll...'). Playing the game is essentially a group activity. Groupwork can be an excellent preliminary activity to class discussion. If one pupil from each group explains their group's results, subsequent comment and criticism can be directed to the group, reducing any personal threat, while offering the prospects of shared success.

Getting groups going

The theme of this volume is *assessment*. Nevertheless, since groupwork is a rather rare activity in classrooms in secondary schools, some guidance on getting started will be offered here. Much fuller guidance is offered in the Red and Blue Boxes, and in the Joint Matriculation Board's Numeracy Modules. Personal experiences of groupwork are an essential starting point. Anyone who has not worked on a mathematical problem in a group for some time should revisit this experience before setting such activities for a class. The problems set out in an earlier chapter (pp. 88, 110 and 117) – Climbing Game, Motor Racing or Consecutive Sums – could be chosen. A note should be made of what each group member is doing at regular intervals (say every three minutes). After 20 minutes, it is appropriate to hold a discussion focused on the following.

- Roles adopted – were some people passive and others active? Who interacted with whom?
- Strategies used – did the group: plan before acting; monitor progress; try simple cases; record results; work systematically?
- What advice would the group have wanted from a teacher – an answer; some hints; questions about progress?
- How often would such advice have been welcome – every five minutes; right at the start, and then at the end?
- What were the best and the worst things about working together?
- How did individuals feel working in the group – confident; threatened; exposed?

Pupils are human, too. Your feelings and theirs are likely to be similar. Personal experiences of groupwork can be used to shape classroom management, the help provided to groups and individuals and the classroom climate promoted during groupwork.

Describing groupwork

The assessment of groupwork needs to begin with statements about the aspects of groupwork which are desirable, and those which are not. As has been argued throughout, the classroom teacher is the person who must make these judgements and then act upon them. First, to refine them into a scheme which can be used in class to observe groups at work, and secondly as the basis for a plan of action to improve the performance both of individuals and of groups. To illustrate this process, a dialect of PROBS (Problem Solving Observation Schedule) will be described. It is just one of many observation schemes, several more of which are described in Open University (1980), and in Ridgway (1988b). PROBS is a tool kit for observing mathematics lessons, which was developed with a number of purposes in mind. In particular, it was designed as a descriptive system which could be customized to provide:

• a tool for teachers to use to analyse problem solving and groupwork in their own classrooms;
• a classroom observation tool for use in curriculum development;
• a research tool to describe in fine detail the activities which take place when people tackle unfamiliar problems (especially in groups);
• a means of communication about important aspects of mathematical education (since the things one chooses to record are implicitly (and hopefully explicitly) also the things one values).

Implicit in the lists of negative and positive aspects of groupwork described earlier are ideas about those aspects of pupil behaviour which are to be encouraged, and those which are to be discouraged. Also implicit is a theory about successful modes of operation when solving problems. This will be made explicit here, and justified elsewhere (Ridgway, 1987).

Figure 8.1 illustrates the collection of intellectual tools which are necessary for succesful problem solving. The *problem space* is the solver's internal representation of the problem, and is rather like a blackboard on which the solver has written down goals, things that are given, ideas to try out, and so on. Since this is an internal representation, its contents cannot be known exactly, although clues can be obtained from things the solver says and writes down.

The solver's resources are the things that can be brought to bear to help solution; these include a wide variety of mathematical knowledge. Here, three aspects of this knowledge are categorized: the knowledge base i.e., the collection of facts, skills and conceptual structures which the individual has; the control structure which the solver employs – knowledge of plans, tactics, heuristics and

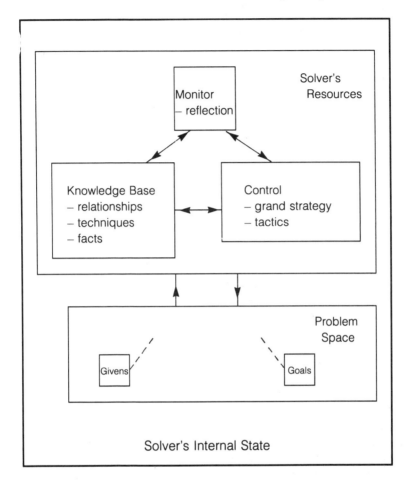

Figure 8.1: Minimum requirements for a model of human problem solving

grand strategies; and the solver's monitor – the source of decisions about how often to review progress, and how to deploy resources.

Too often, the focus of mathematical education has been to enrich the knowledge base at the expense of other components. A rich knowledge base can be used to solve familiar problems quickly without recourse to either monitor or control; knowledge of facts, skills and relationships alone, however, are almost useless for tackling unfamiliar problems. Unfamiliar problems require the deployment of appropriate technique; control skills and the ability to monitor progress are essential to success. If pupils are to acquire such skills, these skills must become a focus for teaching and evaluation. Pupils can be taught how to use heuristics, that is, problem solving tactics which aren't guaranteed to work, but which often result in success, such as 'try simple cases' and 'choose different representations'. They need practise at such tasks on their own. They also need to be made aware of the benefits of such skills by experiencing their 'pay-off'. Integration of heuristics into plans and the need to monitor the problem solving process at regular intervals are also important skills. Groupwork provides an excellent environment to foster this sort of intellectual development, because pupils themselves spontaneously make both monitoring remarks ('what a mess', 'we're getting nowhere') and planning remarks ('let's write things out in order', 'let's try to look at it from a different angle'). Discussion about the need to plan and to review progress can then follow naturally from pupils' own remarks.

Coding events

The following scheme is offered as a basis on which a personal (or departmental) classroom observation schedule might be built. It offers a structure for observation which can be tailored to suit particular purposes. The record sheet shown in Table 8.1 illustrates the overall design.

The obvious features of the record sheet are its appearance as a music score with rows devoted to individual pupils, and columns devoted to resources and time-keeping, as well as to pupil behaviour. A larger space is allocated to record progress on the particular problem and for odd comments, interesting student remarks, and the like. Time and resources (teacher produced material; work cards; calculator; computer; dice...) need little explanation. Behaviour is described at three levels: gross features of the session which are called episodes; processes, which define activities like 'getting started', 'summing up' etc; and events which describe the fine detail of the group work.

EPISODES: might be classified as:
1. exposition;
2. consolidation;
3. discussion;
4. practical work;
5. problem solving;
6. investigation; and as
7. on-task or off-task.

Table 8.1: PROBS record sheet

Date:
Sheet No.

	Observer	Pupils	Lesson	PROBS

Resources (time)	Action: Talk, Qualifiers, Events, Episodes
T	
1	
2	
3	
M	
T	
1	
2	
3	
M	
T	
1	
2	
3	
M	
T	
1	
2	
3	
M	
T	
1	
2	
3	
M	

PROCESSES: are inferred from events and are written on the page when observation has finished. These categories must reflect personal beliefs about the processes involved, and are likely to be closely linked with the particular problem under discussion. Therefore no advice about how to cluster events will be offered.

EVENTS: are the individual things that happen. For the purposes of illustration this discussion will focus solely on conversation. For each event, it is useful to record: who said it; the nature of the utterance; the focus of the utterance; its correctness; and its fate.

WHO SAID IT? Each pupil is represented by a line on the record sheet and each utterance is recorded there. Lines are drawn to join connected events, so conversations are easy to spot.

WHAT WAS SAID? Utterances might be classified as:

r   reasoning (including h hypotheses and d deductions);
s   suggestions for action;
i   information (including e explanations and x examples);
q   questions (including ch checking questions);
a   assertions.

FOCI:
F   facts, skills;
S   structures, relationships;
P   planning;
M   monitoring, reflection.

CORRECTNESS:
√   correct;
0   irrelevant;
x   wrong.
FATE:
z̵   ignored;
c   confirmed;
c̄   contradicted.

Different remarks are then coded by some combination of these symbols.
Some examples:

I'm stuck $a_M^{\surd}$
Why don't we try simple cases s_p or qs_p

'How did you get that?	qr_F or qi_F
What are you trying to do?	q_p
Let's try it for four cubes	s_p
Four is prime	a_F^x
We tried that before and it doesn't work	r_F' or a_F'
Look – triangular numbers; Nonsense!	$r\,\bar{c}_s$

The non-uniqueness of codes shows that the context of an utterance determines its meaning.

Teacher contributions can be noted either by allocating a line to the teacher, or simply by adding a prefix of T; e.g. 'play it a few times to see what happens' is Ts_p. Emotional aspects can be coded by adding + or − to any description; e.g., 'great idea' is $a+$; 'wally' is $a-$.

Despite the apparent complexity of this scheme, most people want to extend the category system once they get used to using it (for example, if one were keen to foster particular process skills like 'specializing' and 'generalizing' a code might be associated with each; one might want codes for the clarity of utterances, or want separate codes for headings aggregated earlier, like 'monitoring and reflection'; actions like: reading; drawing; pointing; measuring; cutting... could be coded). The overall aim should be to develop a scheme which is simple enough to use in class, and yet complex enough to capture events of interest. As skills increase, the desire for finer descriptions are likely to increase, too!

Using the descriptions

What can one do with the results of these observations and descriptions? The most obvious features of these records are: the number of contributions made by different individuals; the flow between them, and the sequence of problem solving episodes. Understanding the nature of the session, in terms of the control of intellectual (and social and emotional) activities, requires some analysis. Once one is familiar with some scheme, this can be done with pupils, from the raw records, immediately after the events have taken place. In the initial stages, it may be necessary to do some analysis before a discussion with a group, although this has the twin disadvantages that it takes up time outside lessons, and that feedback to pupils is delayed, so that the events being discussed will no longer be fresh in the mind.

Discussions with groups

WHAT MATHEMATICAL RESULTS WERE PRODUCED?

Since this is the main focus of mathematics lessons, it is the natural place to begin a discussion. Different pupils can be asked to describe what the group now knows that wasn't known before. One should try hard to listen to what is *said*, not to what one wants to *hear*. A useful strategy is to choose as group speaker the pupil judged to be weakest (or anyone who seems to have been left out of the groupwork by the others). Hopefully, pupils will soon become aware of this device, and will try to overcome this 'unfair' strategy by keeping everyone in touch with findings. The first description of findings produced should not necessarily be accepted. An alternative to try is 'bouncing back'. When pupils offer a page of working, by way of explanation, they can be asked to describe it simply, in words; when they offer a garbled explanation, one can simply repeat it back, verbatim, without intonation – the commonest pupil response is to offer a much improved explanation. The ability to communicate clearly about mathematics is a desirable skill which is hard to develop without practice! This introductory discussion can lead naturally into talk about specialization; ('suppose I had a thousand and five like that – how would you work it out then?'), generalization; ('what else do you think this will work for?'), reasoning: ('tell me why you think that') and proof; ('how would you convince someone that this will always be true?').

HOW WERE THESE RESULTS PRODUCED?

It is useful to ask pupils to reconstruct their discovery processes. What did they do; what records were kept; where did ideas come from; what ideas were generated and ignored; what ideas were tried out and found to be unsuccessful; what led up to good ideas; what blockages were encountered; how were blockages overcome (if at all); was time wasted down blind alleys; what will they do next time? The list isn't exhaustive; it simply provides a few starting points to initiate discussions about mathematical process.

After a few review sessions in which pupils are asked such questions, they will begin to think about such issues as they solve problems. A sign of successful teaching is when pupils ask such questions of themselves and of each other as they work ('what are we doing now'; 'what have we done so far'; 'why are we doing this'; 'what will we do with this result when we get it'?).

REMEDIATING GROUP PROCESSES

A characteristic of groups which are unfamiliar with problem solving activities is an absence of remarks at either the planning level or at the reflective level. Pupils work at the level of facts and skills, and relationships without taking an overview of either where they are going or trying to go, or how well they are progressing. This can be illustrated to pupils by sketching a time line of their work based on observational records, like the one shown in Figure 8.2.

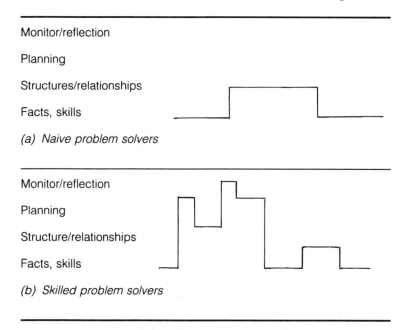

Monitor/reflection

Planning

Structures/relationships

Facts, skills

(a) Naive problem solvers

Monitor/reflection

Planning

Structure/relationships

Facts, skills

(b) Skilled problem solvers

Figure 8.2: Levels of problem solving over time

If groups (or individuals) fail to rise to higher levels (planning, reflection) their progress is likely to be impeded. Bursts of planning are desirable; so too are regular reflections on progress. Work which is dominated by reflection and planning is likely to be as unsuccessful as work where neither occurs. Omissions at any level are significant, and need to be remediated. Notice that on this simple scheme, planning encompasses the use of heuristics, as well as grand strategy. An individual teacher might want to identify each of these in his or her own scheme, if problem solving techniques such as 'be systematic', 'try simple cases', 'work back from the answer', 'think of a related problem', have been introduced. Of course gaps in technique and factual knowledge can also be detected by observation, and can be remedied (although usually these gaps will have been detected already).

This sort of analysis and discussion is not just a frill to add on to didactic teaching; it provides an important vehicle to bring about pupil reflection about themselves as mathematicians, and about the nature of mathematical processes. Such activities are directly analogous to some approaches taken to diagnostic teaching; pupils discuss errors and misconceptions and try to remediate them. Here, it is their overall approach to solving problems which is the target for analysis and remediation. Pupils are encouraged to take the intellectual initiative when faced with unfamiliar tasks. The purpose of the activity is to encourage pupil autonomy; one hopes to help pupils to view their problem solving skills as objects for analysis and discussion – so they can be brought to discuss their knowledge, their plans, and their self monitoring quite naturally, and to improve their overall performance systematically by trying to improve each. This activity is, perhaps, the best possible exemplar of Assessment objective 3.15.

The result of discussions and negotiations with the group, based on observational records, should be some behavioural targets for future groupwork. Obvious contenders are: more monitoring of progress; more formal approaches to planning lines of attack; improved recording of results, and more checking of technical accuracy. There is little point in announcing these objectives; pupils must see the need for them themselves, and agree to try to improve in one or two domains. Pupils' groupwork must not be dominated by a large collection of objectives imposed by the teacher, which they have to achieve at the same time as they work on unfamiliar challenges; such dominance can come to distort the activity as a whole, rather than augment it.

SOCIAL ASPECTS OF PERFORMANCE

The major foci of attention here are the nature of the utterances, who makes them (e.g. whether all group members are making a contribution), and the fate of the utterances. Group profiles can be constructed in terms of each focus: i.e. the nature of the utterances (assertions, suggestions, explanations, questions, reasoning and managerial remarks); by noting down who makes each remark; and by recording the responses (ignored; confirmed; contradicted; bounced back). These records then form the basis for a discussion with the group; are enough suggestions for action collected before work proceeds? Are one or two members doing all the planning (or, indeed, everything)? Do some group members contribute nothing? Do some pupils try to contribute, but have all their suggestions ignored? Particular roles being played by group members might be identified, such as: recorder; artist; calculator; manager. One device to encourage the integration of isolated pupils is to allocate specific roles such as 'recorder' or 'group speaker'. As before, the purpose of the discussion with the group is to set some behavioural goals for group members to aim for. These can be task orientated: 'make sure everyone makes at least one suggestion about how to start, before you touch your calculators', or 'generate at least three simple cases before you produce any hypotheses'; or socially orientated 'ask for an explanation before you contradict a suggestion'; 'just use one biro and take turns, so that you are forced to work together'. Again, pupils must not be overwhelmed with 'outside' tasks when they work.

EMOTIONAL ASPECTS OF PERFORMANCE

It is easy to inhibit good groupwork. Adopting a bullying posture; ignoring contributions; commenting adversely about the quality of others' ideas, or the nature of the task are all effective ploys. Each of these can be recognized from the coding of a superscripted minus sign; emotionally supportive remarks are also easily recognized. A less obvious thing to be aware of is the handling of suggestions and hypotheses. Creative problem solving is facilitated when pupils feel free to be wrong. A phase of generating hypotheses and ideas is essential; criticism, deduction and analysis in this phase will inhibit the flow of ideas, and should be avoided. Inhibition of ideas is likely to characterize groups whose records show short cycles of hypothesis generation and contradiction, rather than a long phase of hypothesis generation followed by reasoning which includes contradictions. One can distinguish between these two phases (creation, evaluation) in discussions with pupils. Pupils can be asked to air their feelings publicly about being wrong; many people inhibit the flow of their ideas to avoid being wrong. The need to inhibit critical thought during phases of idea generation, and the importance of mutual support, should be emphasized.

The purpose of this discussion with the group is to give them a language to handle processes of which they are (usually) dimly aware. Working in groups can make pupils vulnerable to others' criticisms in ways which they are not vulnerable in other forms of teaching. It is the task of the teacher to defend pupils against these dangers ('why did you say that – do you think it is helpful?', 'how would you feel if I had said that to you?', 'don't analyze hypotheses until you have generated a few more', 'don't just knock the hypothesis – try and amend it, or find a better one', 'every great idea in mathematics started out as a conjecture – not all conjectures will end up as great ideas, but you won't get anywhere unless you try out some good guesses').

COGNITIVE, SOCIAL AND EMOTIONAL ASPECTS

Separate headings have been used to illustrate three major components of groupwork. Of course, they are mutually dependent, like the three components on a clover leaf; none can be ignored if the whole is to be understood.

Discussions with individuals

Discussions with individuals proceed in much the same way as discussions with groups, although the emphasis will be somewhat different.

WHAT MATHEMATICAL RESULTS WERE PRODUCED?

Individual interviews are time consuming; a modest goal is to talk to each pupil at least once per term about some mathematics they have produced. It is appropriate to ask for explanations of results before reading any written work. If questions ask explicitly for explanations ('justify your results'), it is worth hearing a verbal summary; aspects of the explanation that need improvement can be probed gently; one might ask for repeated explanations ('I'm sorry, I don't understand – can you say it in a different way?', 'I think I see what you mean – how would you explain it to someone coming fresh to the problem?'); written explanations can be read aloud, slowly. Almost everyone finds it easier to express themselves orally than in writing; pupils will usually be dissatisfied with their efforts, and will want to rewrite their explanation (especially if your gentle coaching has been successful). They should be encouraged to do so, and then to read revisions aloud before deciding on the final form.

The explanation will raise a number of topics for discussion, in particular, about the logical consistency of conclusions; alternative hypotheses considered; ways in which results were justified; ideas for new developments, and the like. Discussions with the teacher complement discussions with fellow pupils; the teacher can be both more naive (please say that again – I didn't grasp it the first time) and more sophisticated ('what will you try next?', 'does this result remind you of anything else you have come across?') than a peer. Conversational style can be tailored to the needs perceived.

HOW WERE THESE RESULTS PRODUCED?

Pupils can be asked to reconstruct the work that took place, and to identify their own roles. Records taken of their contribution in terms of their utterances can be shared. The purposes of this discussion are to: shift the balance in the nature of the utterances made (usually to include some monitoring and planning remarks); to make pupils aware of the kinds of contribution they might make (asking for information; generating hypotheses and suggestions for action); and, overall, to make pupils aware of their current balance of skills as group members. This discussion can be used to set individual behavioural goals. ('Before the end of term, try to make at least one clearly articulated contribution to a class discussion. If you don't think the group is getting anywhere, say so – and ask for a new plan').

SOCIAL ASPECTS OF PERFORMANCE

Ask about the pupil's view of him or herself as a group member, in terms of the amount contributed personally (too much or too little) and the value of these contributions as judged by the group. Is groupwork enjoyable; and how could the group be made to function better? Again, the purpose is to agree on some changes that the individual might make to personal behaviour in the group.

EMOTIONAL ASPECTS OF PERFORMANCE

One might ask about things that make working in groups both most, and least, satisfying. What does the pupil feel the benefit of groupwork to be (if anything!)? How can the emotional climate of the group be improved? Of course, classroom observations will have highlighted pupils who are a major source of positive and negative emotional remarks. Pupils who make a high proportion of negative remarks most need to be persuaded of the need to reform, and need some pointers about how to do it. ('Don't knock an idea unless you have got a better one'; 'when you have a good idea, introduce it as a suggestion not an assertion').

COGNITIVE, SOCIAL AND EMOTIONAL ASPECTS.

As noted before, these headings are not independent. The purpose of this discussion is to make pupils aware of group processes, roles, and individual social behaviour, and to think about ways in which things can be changed in order to function better as mathematicians.

Summative evaluations of performance in groups

Earlier discussion has focused on the assessment of groupwork for formative purposes; the primary intention has been to help pupils improve their performance in groups. Next come some suggestions for ways in which these formative descriptions can be tailored to produce a summative statement.

Assessing mathematical outcomes

Pupils can be asked to write up the results of their groupwork individually (or to explain it orally, in the case of pupils with writing difficulties). There will be pronounced differences in the quality of the work produced, their understanding of results, reporting of progress, and the like. The knowledge that individual writing will be required can itself be a strong motivation for pupils to engage in the tasks in hand, and to ensure that they understand the work being done.

Assessing an individual's performance in groups

An important issue of any statement of achievement concerns the nature of the behaviour observed, the way it is sampled, and the other situations to which it generalizes. This is obvious in most areas of mathematics, although not much discussed; it is less obvious when one deals with processes and social aspects of mathematics. Consider a statement like 'displays skills in arithmetic'. One would be unlikely to make such a judgement on the basis of a single observation of a pupil doing just one sum. One would want to define a range of components (different operations; integers, fractions and decimals), and would probably want to define a minimum number of items for each combination on which 'skill' would have to be demonstrated. One would also be rather modest in any claims for the generalizations which could be made for the grand summary statement. Most pupils have technical skills which they can display in contexts closely similar to those in which they were learned, but which they cannot generalize to other contexts ('choice of operation' – knowing when to divide, add, etc. in the case of arithmetic skills). The same remarks can be made about skills which are displayed when working in groups. A blanket statement like 'displays skills in groupwork' is as uninformative as its counterpart in arithmetic, and needs similar qualification. The skills displayed need to be described (emotionally supportive; generates good ideas; explains clearly; offers plans ...); the sources of evidence need to be clear (written work, observations of groupwork, interviews); the pattern of sampling must be explicit (informally observed once; systematic observation schedule used on occasions when the pupil was working in six different groups); the nature of the tasks being performed must be stated (problem solving in pure mathematics; discussions of graphical work ...). Generalization of this evidence is probably best left to the reader. While one can argue plausibly that pupils who cannot show skills in groupwork in class are unlikely to be able to show them outside, it doesn't follow that pupils who can work effectively in class in groups will be able to perform well in groups of different composition (older, younger, more knowledgeable, less knowledgeable) working on different tasks. Statements about what has been achieved in groupwork, therefore, need very careful wording. 'Can make a useful contribution to a working group' requires only an existence proof: on one occasion the pupil did or said something useful (wrote down results; had a blinding insight that changed the whole approach). 'Is a valuable group member in class' implies that the pupil has been seen to make valuable contributions to a number of different groups; the nature of these contributions, and the supporting evidence should be available to the reader. 'Will be a valuable member of any group' is a prediction, not an observation, and will, almost certainly, be wrong.

9 Assessing Practical Work in Mathematics

Practical work is generally viewed as being fundamental to the development of mathematical understanding in the early years of primary school. In secondary school, however, it attracts rather less attention. The Cockcroft Report asserts that '... pupils of all levels of attainment can benefit from the opportunity for appropriate practical experience'; practical work is one of Cockcroft's 'missing activities'.

The National Criteria for Mathematics list practical work amongst their aims, and practical work is featured as one of the two objectives which must be realized in all schemes by 1991. Its assessment poses a number of problems, which will be addressed in this chapter, notably:

- what *is* practical work in mathematics;
- why should it be fostered;
- how can it be assessed;
- how can practical work be integrated into classroom activities?

What is practical mathematics?

Every one of the Assessment Objectives can be involved in practical mathematics; several can only be assessed via practical mathematics. So what is it? A number of distinct meanings are given to the phrase. Here are some of them:

- work constructing things: scissors and geometrical instruments must be used to make objects which require the exercise of mathematical skills, e.g. technique in using these instruments, as well as exercising concepts concerned with spatial relationships such as notions of nets and geometry and aesthetics;

• using apparatus to illustrate mathematical concepts: apparatus such as Cuisinere rods, containers of different shapes which are used to transfer water, balances and the like, all illustrate mathematical ideas, relationships and operations;

• empirical work: the techniques involved in observing systematically and in carrying out experiments are the hallmark of scientific activity. Skills are concerned with obtaining knowledge through direct observation and experimentation, in order to provide mathematical data and patterns for analysis and display;

• mathematics based on everyday situations: such problems may well be tackled more easily by the use of some mathematical technique. There need be no equipment used other than paper and pencil in tackling such practical problems. Examples are decision-making, planning, design tasks and resource allocation tasks. Hugh Burkhardt has offered a classification of this latter class of practical problems, as follows: action problems where solutions can affect everyday behaviour 'how can I reconcile homework, the TV, and my paper round?'; believable problems where pupils see that they are action problems for the future, or for someone they identify with 'should I go for a job in London (...Isle of Skye)?'; curious problems which are inherently intriguing, or intriguing in their methods of solution, 'why are there two high tides each day?'; educational problems illustrate principles which are educationally important, even though the context may be dubious. 'If great-great-grandmama had invested a pound in 1900 for each of her great-great-grandchildren, at five per cent annual interest, what would we each receive now?'; dubious problems simply offer an exercise in mathematical technique, set in a concrete, rather than abstract, setting.

Professor Burkhardt comments '... mathematical education has rarely aimed above the Curious and is very largely Dubious'. Increased emphasis on practical mathematics is an attempt to remedy this state of affairs.

One of the main reasons for the analysis of practical situations is the belief that mathematics has a role to play in solving problems that pupils face (or will face) outside the classroom. A few characteristics of such problems can be identified:

- they arise naturally in the world – no one has to invent them;
- pupils judge how they are to be addressed (analyzed logically, ignored, referred to experts...);
- pupils have to live with the results of their decisions and actions (they don't just forget them once the analysis has been done);
- mathematics is used only in so far as it helps with the problem; the nature of the problem determines the weight placed on mathematical, social, emotional aspects, when deciding what to do;
- there is rarely a single right answer; the 'best' answer depends heavily on local circumstances;
- there is rarely a best method;
- time available for solution is usually quite long – days and weeks rather than 30 minutes.

These characteristics are not shared with many of the mathematical questions set to children.

Why teach practical mathematics?

Practical mathematics almost never occurs in representative secondary school classrooms. If pupils are to use mathematical skills outside the classroom, some practical work inside them is essential (of course, classroom practical mathematics will not guarantee use outside). If pupils are to use mathematics when engaged in construction tasks, mending cycles, decorating or cooking, they need experience in integrating their mathematical skills with their 'performance' skills. A multi-faceted approach to learning is likely to lead to a well integrated framework of mathematical concepts, which is hard to achieve via other means. Practical mathematics should be taught:

- to show the utility of mathematics in everyday situations;
- to increase the range of methods which pupils can bring to bear on problems;
- because the techniques to be acquired in order to construct objects from card, transparent film etc. – using geometrical instruments and cutting precisely, are instrumentally valuable;
- because the use of 'apparatus' tasks provides other means of mathematical expression, to complement written and oral

forms, thereby widening the potential for aesthetic appeal and sensory pleasure in mathematics learning;
- to provide situations for concrete operational thinking before symbolic thinking takes place; e.g. exploring the relationship between the perimeters of rectangular figures, and the area of the figures can readily be done via the presentation of square tiles or loops of string which are deformed into various rectangles;
- to introduce the skills of mathematical modelling into the classroom (see Assessment Objective 3.15: respond to a problem relating to a relatively unstructured situation by translating it into an appropriately structured form);
- to present wholistic tasks so that children can practise strategic skills and must select the mathematical techniques they choose to use.

How can practical mathematics be assessed?

The APU surveys

The Assessment of Performance Unit of the Department of Education and Science (DES) has a great deal of experience in test design, administration and evaluation of some aspects of practical mathematics. An excellent introduction to the conduct and assessment of practical tasks is provided by the APU teachers' booklet *Assessing Practical Mathematics in Secondary Schools* (Foxman, 1987).

The National Foundation for Educational Research has carried out a number of major surveys for the APU; the practical surveys were carried out between 1978 and 1982. The target groups studied were 11-year-olds in their last year of Junior School and 15-year-olds in their first term of 5th year Secondary School. As well as their extensive knowledge concerning the construction and administration of practical tasks, the APU has a rich body of data concerning the facility levels of different practical tasks. All this knowledge provides an important starting point for anyone concerned with practical testing in their own classrooms.

The administration of the APU tests had a number of interesting features:

- tests were presented orally by a tester to individual pupils who were then expected to carry out activities and report their progress orally for the most part;
- on several tasks, pupils were asked to describe their plans before starting work on the task; after completing the task they were often asked to describe what they had done.

The earlier surveys (1978 and 1979) were largely focused on the use of apparatus and materials intended to assess practical skills in measuring and constructing, as well as pupils' understanding of numerical and spatial concepts. From 1980 onwards a broader view of practical mathematics was taken; everyday concepts were included such as planning journeys and organizing parties as were other problem solving topics, for example the conduct of investigations.

A wide range of pupil skills are assessed implicitly by these tasks; there was no attempt to focus on the assessment of a specific skill or single concept but rather to look at more general processes. For example, tests concerned with planning a journey required pupils to read timetables and menus, to understand maps and to discover the costs of visiting different places. These skills were embedded in larger tasks which involved decision making and general planning, and in which pupils had to take account of the constraints on time and money. In problem solving involving pure mathematics, apparatus such as rods or tiles were used to explore mathematical relationships. Again, a variety of process skills were required to solve these problems including: working systematically; conjecturing; using trial and error methods, reasoning, being systematic, checking and generalizing.

SOME EXAMPLES OF THE APU TESTING AND RESULTS

The categories of practical work tested in the APU surveys between 1978 and 1982 (Foxman, 1987) are shown below:

Concepts and skills

(i)   Measuring and constructing
        – estimating (lengths, areas, volumes of objects and shapes)

- using measuring instruments (ruler, protractor, balance)
- other measuring tasks (area, volume/capacity, mass)
- using measuring and geometrical instruments to construct 2D shapes and 3D models

(ii) Using apparatus to demonstrate understanding of particular ideas or concepts
- symmetry (mirror, folding and cutting paper)
- fractions and ratio (rods, nails and other lengths)
- visualising (2D diagrams of 3D models)

(iii) Calculator skills
- direct assessment of skills (checking, order of operations, approximation, successive approximation)
- optional use of calculator in larger tasks requiring computation

Problem solving

(iv) 'Everyday' planning and problem solving
- planning journeys and trips
- designing a kitchen
- organising a party

(v) Using apparatus to assist thinking about investigations
- arrangements of rods of given length
- perimeter and area of configurations of square tiles

All the tasks are presented orally and pupils may be asked to talk about or explain:
- how a task will be attempted
- what methods were used to obtain an answer
- what rules or relationships are involved
- the mathematical ideas and concepts involved

These categories will be illustrated by three examples: understanding line symmetry; calculator skills; and appreciation of number pattern.

LINE SYMMETRY: Figure 9.1 shows some of the problems used to investigate pupils' understanding of line symmetry, along with the performance of pupils on these tasks.

Clear guidelines were laid down to define 'reasonable attempt' in terms of the position of the fold line and the size, shape, position and symmetry of the diamond on the paper.

Figure 9.1: Understanding line symmetry

Pupil and tester have similar sheets of paper (⅓ A4).

Pupil has pencil (no ruler).

"I want you to watch while I fold and cut my piece of paper."

"This piece of paper was like yours before I folded it and cut a piece out of it. Draw on your piece of paper what this will look like when it's opened out. Draw the fold line as well."

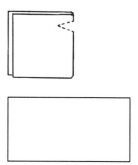

Results	Boys	Girls	Total
	%	%	%
* Reasonable attempt	62	46	54
Clearly incorrect in 1 or more aspects	27	38	33
Draws small version of pattern	5	4	4
Other	4	4	4
Pupil's work not returned	2	8	5

Present and plain ⅓ A4 sheet.

"Fold and cut your piece of paper so that you see this pattern when it's unfolded again."

Some of the methods used to obtain this symmetrical pattern

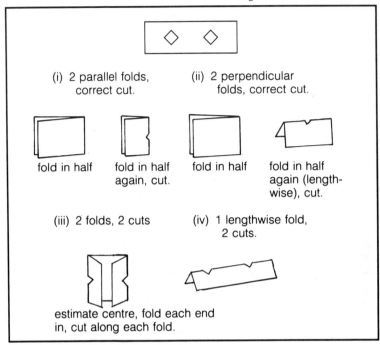

(i) 2 parallel folds,
     correct cut.

(ii) 2 perpendicular
      folds, correct cut.

fold in half

fold in half
again, cut.

fold in half

fold in half
again (length-
wise), cut.

(iii) 2 folds, 2 cuts

(iv) 1 lengthwise fold,
      2 cuts.

estimate centre, fold each end
in, cut along each fold.

Present sheet and ruler.

"Draw the positions of the mirror where the pattern remains the same."
Present mirror
"You can use the mirror if you like."

Sixty per cent of boys, but only 51 per cent of girls, drew three lines correctly.

CALCULATOR SKILLS: competence in the use of an electronic calculator is becoming an increasingly important skill and is specified as Assessment Objective 3.5 'use an electronic calculator'. The use of a calculator enables one to assess pupils' abilities to estimate results, use checking procedures for answers obtained via alternative methods, assess their understanding of the calculator display and their interpretation of decimals (e.g. that in a calculation involving money an answer of 13.5 means £13 and 50p). Items from the APU written survey are shown in Figure 9.2.

A number of interesting results emerged.

- While pupils were happy to round a decimal number up or down to a whole number when appropriate, they were much less willing to round a whole number to the nearest 10 or 100.
- About 70 per cent of pupils were able to check division or subtraction by using the inverse operation, although only half

Item	Success rate	Item	Success rate
$112 \div 7$	84%	$9.6 \div 4$	77%
$\dfrac{112}{7}$	69%	$\dfrac{9.6}{4}$	60%

Figure 9.2: Calculator skills

of the pupils were able to say clearly what result was expected when this inverse operation was carried out.
- When asked to work out a calculation such as:
$$\frac{17.86 \times 154.3}{10.9}$$
almost 20 per cent of the sample asked what the fraction line meant.
- Faced with the sum:
$$16.7 + \frac{14.98}{5.1} \times 102$$
only 15 per cent of pupils obtained the correct answer; about a third of pupils simply entered the number and operations from left to right.
- In a calculation which required pupils to calculate the total cost of 36 items at £14.50 each most pupils (92 per cent) obtained the correct number in the calculating display but only 35 per cent could interpret it correctly (a further 35 per cent gave the response 520.2 without reference to pounds and pence: 13 per cent read the display as £52 and 2p; five per cent gave the answer £52.02).
- When calculators were allowed when tackling other problems, for example those concerned with the day trip, some pupils were reluctant to use them – viewing it as cheating.
- 'The calculator questions have revealed that about one third of the 15-year-olds could use a calculator competently for a range of computations. Others had difficulties with computational skills such as approximating, rounding and knowing the order in which a series of operations should be carried out. Other weaknesses related to misinterpreting the display and a lack of knowledge of notation.'

This last point is illustrated by performance on the problem in Figure 9.3.

Best Buy: Using a calculator

Washing-up liquid

Which size of washing-up liquid is better value for money?
CALCULATOR ALLOWED.

ANSWER: *38%* correct

53% other option – incorrect

9% do not give a final answer

METHOD: *23%* compare volume/penny or cost/ml

41% double the cost of the small size and then judge between 1080 ml @ 62p and 1000 ml @ 60p; or halve 1 litre and compare 500 ml @ 30p with 540 ml @ 31p

5% suggest that bigger sizes are always better value

4% guess

2% compare ratio of prices to volumes – 540 : 1000 or 31 : 60

1% compare cost/litre

15% give answers coded as "other"

24% give rough estimates and are asked if they can "work it out exactly"

7% need prompting as to the number of ml in a litre

Figure 9.3: Weaknesses in calculator skills

These poor results may arise because of pupil assumptions that the larger quantity will provide better value for money, and these assumptions are not disproved by the calculations they perform.

AWARENESS OF NUMBER PATTERNS: the tasks below illustrate the APU tasks and facility levels for a number of their problem solving tasks focused on areas and perimeters.

Remove 3 tiles from the bag.
"This is an investigation about making shapes with these tiles and counting the distance around the outside for each shape. The tiles can only be joined edge to edge (demonstrate with 2 tiles ▢▢) *or corner to corner* (demonstrate ▢▢)."

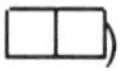

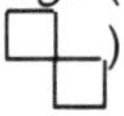

Make this arrangement ▢▢▢ 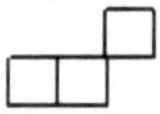
"If we say that each edge is one unit long, what is the distance round the outside of this arrangement?" Trace the outline with your finger.

Results
80% gave the correct answer without prompting
14% gave the correct answer after the prompt
The remainder were shown what was required.

Present 4th tile.
"Arrange these 4 tiles so that the distance round the outside is as small as possible. Write your answer in the table."

Results
70% gave the correct answer without prompting

25% gave ▢▢▢▢

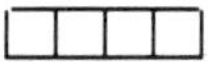

After the prompt an additional *24%* were successful.

"Can you give me a rule for finding the largest distance round the outside for any number of tiles?"

Results
40% said 'Times by 4' or 'Multiply by 4'
21% said 'Add 4 each time' or 'Goes up in 4's'
23% referred to how tiles were arranged
After the prompts, a further *17%* gave 'Times/multiply by 4'.

Figure 9.4: Awareness of number patterns

GENERAL ISSUES

Are practical tasks appropriate for pupils of all age groups?

'The practical test results suggested that there were aspects of each topic which challenged above average attainers, but that lower attainers sometimes used more appropriate methods than those with apparently stronger theoretical knowledge.'

Testers consistently pointed to the 15-year-olds' unfamiliarity with practical mathematics. This was particularly marked in higher attaining pupils. Students commonly commented that they preferred being able to use materials that they could handle.

Another feature of the survey was that pupils particularly enjoyed the tests. This may be attributable to its novel aspects, but is plausibly related to the nature of the tasks themselves.

Reviewing the APU practical surveys

The APU practical survey provokes thoughts about: the nature of the tasks; pupil performance; different forms of test administration; training of administrators; and, most importantly, the implications for curriculum and classroom practice.

THE NATURE OF THE TASKS: generally speaking, the tasks used were significantly different from conventional mathematics problems. As well as the obvious difference that the focus was on practical mathematics, problems were often set and responded to orally. Pupils were frequently asked about plans, and were sometimes given hints. Nevertheless, the range of tasks is far narrower than those implied by the label 'practical mathematics'. In particular, tasks are short and somewhat fragmented; no attempt was made to assess progress on extended pieces of practical mathematics. Tasks, in general, focused on a narrow range of topics in 'everyday' mathematics. Pupils worked individually throughout. (The APU began a further survey in 1987, in which pupils work collaboratively in small groups, solving problems as a team).

PUPIL PERFORMANCE: few pupils had experienced practical mathematics before the survey and so performance levels reflect the amount of transfer of training from conventional mathematics. As with all surveys, there were some surprises (for me, at least!); good performance on reading timetables, for example, and poor performance on the 'best buy' washing-up liquid problem. These data provide a baseline against which we can judge the effects of more exposure to practical mathematics in class.

FORMS OF ADMINISTRATION

The focus of the APU tests is assessment; the main benefactor is the DES and the community concerned with mathematical education. Testing was not carried out for the primary benefit of the pupils and teachers involved. The most direct lessons to be learned from the APU surveys relate to summative, rather than formative, evaluation. What are the advantages and disadvantages of the different forms of administration used?

CLASS TESTS: are appropriate when resources are adequate (in terms of space and apparatus). This is usually the case if the apparatus is physically small, cheap and easy to issue in class. Pupils should require little help; the teacher role should be confined to monitoring the class. It is almost impossible to provide statements of the process skills which pupils display if an entire class is to be observed on a single occasion. Pupil responses will usually be answers or constructions of some sort which can be assessed later. Class tests of this sort are therefore most useful for formal testing of a conventional kind rather than for diagnostic assessment.

PRACTICAL CIRCUSES: are appropriate for formal practical testing when apparatus is in short supply and when each task takes a relatively short amount of time to complete. A series of tasks is set up at stations distributed around the room and a pupil is directed to each station. After a specified time each pupil moves on to a new task according to some plan devised in advance. The advantages of a circus are that more elaborate materials can be used and that students can be tested simultaneously. The disadvantage is that the tasks which are appropriate to this test format are usually those which can be completed rather quickly and so extended pieces of work cannot be tackled. Pupils also face rigid time contraints, although these can be reduced by having more stations than pupils.

INDIVIDUAL INTERVIEWS: are very time consuming but yield rich data about what the student is doing and the skills which they can deploy in particular settings. In the APU surveys up to four topics were set to each pupil, each one consisting of a series of questions centred on a particular topic – for example: planning a day trip; designing a kitchen; the relationship between perimeters and areas. Individual tests require detailed scripts which specify the questions to be asked together with a set of prompts, probes and hints. It is usually appropriate to begin with easy questions at the outset and progress to harder ones. Of course, it is essential to take account of the help given to pupils and to give help in a formalized way. Interviews allow time for extended pupil explanations and reflections which are hard to achieve in a classroom setting. The conduct of individual interviews needs practice if one's pupils are all to receive similar experiences and have their marks assessed to the same standard. The problem is heightened if one wishes to ensure comparability between different testers in different classrooms. The APU approach is to provide a Practical Test Manual (written by Lynn Joffe) together with some videotaped interviews, as well as the apparatus to be used. The APU recruits teachers who are experienced in the teaching of both boys and girls in the age group concerned, and invites every tester to a residential conference which is held a few weeks before the survey takes place. During the two-and-a-half day course testers review and discuss videotaped interviews and adopt the roles of both of tester and pupil. Towards the end of the course, they practice their skills on pupils; after the course they are encouraged to practice the administration of tests with pupils at their own schools (*after* the surveys, testers discuss results and in particular, any problems relating to the test scripts or other aspects of test administration with the APU team).

Implications for classroom practice

The ambitions of class teachers are probably more modest than those of the APU, in terms of the reliability of assessment sought. Nevertheless, there is a general desire to assess pupils in a systematic way and to achieve some rough comparability in the assessments made within school and between schools. The activities of: careful task design; the preparation of an interviewer's script which identifies a scheme for intervention and probing questions; the need to share experiences (probably presented on videotape for viewing with colleagues to focus discussions on the principles of interviewing); the need to practise these skills both in private and in front of one's colleagues; and the need to talk afterwards about the problems which arose; are all important components if an adequate testing procedure is to be developed. Very few people have skills in the assessment of practical tasks. Given the wide range of practical tasks which are possible (it has already been noted that the task definitions used by the APU are rather narrower than those identified in the National Criteria, or those which particular groups of teachers might choose to use) it is clear that time must be found for this process of practice and reflection concerning the nature and nurture or practical activities in class and the ways they can be stimulated and assessed. Teachers, in contrast with the APU, can devote time to individual work over the whole school year. This offers the opportunity to observe the mathematical processes deployed by pupils in detail over an extended period. Such activities as guessing and checking, conjecturing, working systematically and choosing a variety of representations, can be observed. Subsequently, the way the pupil proceeded can be discussed with the pupil in an attempt to improve their overall strategic skills. Derek Foxman comments:

> The value of discussion with pupils, the opportunity to observe pupils tackling the problems was endorsed by over 100 experienced secondary teachers who participated in the five age 15 surveys from 1978 to 1982. Several noted that when pupils manipulate apparatus and talk about what they have done their thinking processes are externalized thus enabling testers to gain a deeper insight into their understanding. In order to derive this benefit, the teacher does have to interview and observe pupils but observing does not need to be done exclusively in a one-to-one situation while discussion can take place with a whole class. (Foxman, 1987.)

Practical work and the curriculum

WHAT EQUIPMENT IS NEEDED?

The NFER review of assessment practices used with low attainers found that secondary school teachers were resistant to the idea of practical work because of the need to purchase, store and maintain the necessary equipment. Such concerns are quite reasonable. Look, however, at the complete list of equipment actually used in the 1980 APU survey. Apparatus is relatively cheap, easily stored and largely reusable. The notable exception to this observation is the balance – but most schools already have balances in science laboratories.

Paper, plain and squared; pencils; calculators; laminated sheets; angles; triangles; protractors; rulers; scissors; mirrors; compasses; shapes in coloured card; plastic tiles; large perspex box; small perspex box; wooden cubes; wooden spheres; tins; maps; string; tape measures; double pan balance; 20g, 50g and 100g masses; plasticine; 1g, 3g and 9g lego masses; 2p and 10p coins; coloured dice; dominoes; ferry charts; and diagrams with information concerning a journey.

To this list we might reasonably add: counters; beer mats; construction straws; lollipop sticks; plastic cups; isometric paper; sheets of card; linking cubes; logiblocks; and lego, all of which are readily available at a modest cost and can form the basis for investigational work and other kinds of practical mathematics.

Getting started

Many school subjects include a practical component, for example the sciences, geography, craft, design and technology and home economics. In mathematics, however, practical work is relatively rare. There is scope for mathematical tasks which cross curriculum boundaries, however, care must be taken to ensure that such tasks are developed in collaboration with subject experts in other disciplines, so that they do not reflect outdated approaches in those other subjects.

In their present form, the formal methods of assessment used by the APU have limited use for classroom teaching. However, with some modifications they can be well suited for classroom use. In class, individual interviews can take place and practical assessment can be based on small groupwork. When the class is working on a range of practical tasks, some time can be spent during each lesson in discussion with individuals or these small groups. Over the course of a term, a reasonable picture can be built up of the practical skills of the entire class. These sessions are likely to be less formal than those used by the APU, but are nevertheless well worthwhile. Extended tasks present the opportunity to discuss progress with every pupil in the class. Such extended tasks offer the opportunity to see a wide range of pupil skills – from the way tasks are planned through to technical accuracy when drawing.

A wide variety of tasks can reasonably be considered to be 'practical mathematics'. Examples below illustrate a number of classroom-based activities which can stimulate practical mathematics. In general, when practising new skills (here, classroom management of an unfamiliar sort) it is as well to begin simply and to leave adventure until later. A good starting point is provided by investigational work based on concrete materials (tiles, counters, folding paper).

PRACTICAL WORK AND INVESTIGATIONS

The Blue Box provides several examples of problems which can be introduced as examples of practical mathematics; so too do the APU surveys. Games provide one set of contexts; problems involving paper folding (e.g. 'how many creases do you get if you fold a piece of paper in half, six times?'), movements of counters, (e.g. 'frogs'), arrangements of tiles and blocks (e.g. 'skeleton towers') provide others. Examples are given on pages 88 and 96 and in Example 10. Suggestions for lesson plans are included in the Blue Box and will not be repeated here.

PRACTICAL WORK CONSTRUCTING THINGS

Construction tasks can focus on technical skills, visualization, following and writing instructions and oral mathematics. Sample activities are to:

- give pupils a drawing on isometric paper of an object they are to construct from linking cubes, or Lego; their task being to draw sections of different sides of the object;
- begin with an object (e.g. a car made out of Lego) and ask pupils to write out instructions on how such an object can be built (actually, two identical objects are needed so that pupils can take one apart without forgetting what it should really be like!); these instructions can then be passed on to another pupil who assembles the object unseen;
- set pupils working in pairs, separated by a screen; one pupil is given a diagram (for example, an arrangement of geometric shapes), the other is equipped with drawing instruments, the pupils' task is to communicate the diagram, unseen; the task can be made easy or hard, depending on the figure chosen; it provides excellent practice in oral skills and technical mathematics;

SORTING

50 red and 50 blue counters are placed alternately in a line across the floor:
RBRBRBR . . . RB

By swapping adjacent counters (see arrows) they have to be sorted into 2 groups, with all the reds at one end and all the blues at the other:
RRR . . . RRRBBB . . . BBB

* What is the *least* number of moves needed to do this?
  How many moves are needed for n red and n blue counters?

* What happens when the counters are placed in different starting formations:
  For example   **RRBBRRBBRRBB . . . RRBB**
  or   **RBBRRBBRRBB . . . RBBR**

* What happens when there are red, blue and green counters arranged
  RBGRBG . . . RBG
  What happens with 4 colours?
  What happens with m colours?

* Invent and explore your own arrangement of counters.
  Write about your findings.

Example 10: Sorting

- design tasks, such as 'produce a packet suitable for use in a sports shop to hold a golf ball'; issues of functionality (what will it cost to make? will packets stack? roll off shelves?) and aesthetics (would I want to buy it?) are left up to the children;
- conduct extended projects, such as the construction of pop-up cards, or boxes, or polyhedra; the numeracy module 'Be a Paper Engineer' supports such activities;
- experiment with plasticine, modelling and measuring various shapes (cylinders, spheres, cones) made from the same lump, can be a useful precursor to discussions of the equation of volumes of different objects (and even to calculus).

PRACTICAL WORK GATHERING DATA

Conducting surveys (of pocket money, hours of television watched, bedtimes, favourite or hated school meals) all provide information useful to children (to get more money, go to bed later, or eat better) while developing critical skills in the conduct and interpretation of surveys. Such skills are useful, as the Financial Times (15 Nov, 1986) illustrates:

British Gas
In the manner made famous by advertisers of cat food the Government's financial advisers tell us that 'research shows over 5m people' (13 per cent of the adult population) 'are currently certain to buy British Gas shares'. In fact 12.8 per cent of a sample of 2,156 adults said they were certain to buy. Cookability, that's the beauty of stats.
It may appear slightly odd that 276 – sorry, 5.25m – people are certain to buy something before they know exactly what the price is...

Other newspaper extracts can form the basis for discussions about sampling, confidence intervals and the public image of statistics.

A number of scientific investigations, whose basic purpose is mathematical modelling, can be done with very simple equipment. For example, 'how is the period of a pendulum affected by: the length of the swing, the length of the string and the mass attached?', Or (for A-level mechanics), take thin cardboard sheets sized A4, A5, A6... and explore the terminal velocity of each when dropped with the face parallel to the ground. Explore the effect of different masses by adding extra sheets. Can pupils model this situation using Newton's laws?

PRACTICAL WORK AND EVERYDAY SITUATIONS

This is undoubtedly the most difficult mathematical challenge to be faced! The number of action problems and believable problems which have been assembled so far is rather small. There is an urgent need for more and some starting points are offered later.

Standard models do have some uses; particular mathematical techniques are often used in economics, medicine and science. Familiarity with such models and the ability to tailor them to particular situations are useful skills. Awareness of such techniques should be part of students' general knowledge about the role played by mathematics in the world. However, pupils are often taught 'standard models' as if they were 'practical mathematics' – examples set on cars rolling down hills might 'ignore all sources of friction' – and so the context does little more than offer a cosmetic gloss to the task of mastering technique.

Mathematical modelling is hard. When pupils are led through standard techniques, the mathematical demands can be quite high. However, when faced with a realistic problem which they have to tackle themselves, using some of the mathematics known to them, pupils can reasonably be expected only to deploy techniques which they have mastered already, because the strategic demands are so high. Effectively, this means that students should be set problems which require no more technical sophistication than they were able to demonstrate, say, three years earlier.

Just as the calculator promises to play a major role in the development of conceptual understanding by removing the technical load imposed by problems, the computer promises to facilitate modelling skills by reducing the need for difficult algebraic manipulations. Generic software such as spreadsheets and modelling packages allow the user to specify quite complex models (e.g. ones that, specified as differential equations, could not be solved analytically) as sets of simple equations which are iterated. Jon Ogborn's Dynamic Modelling System is an example of a system designed for use by pupils. When such programs are used, the activity of modelling then focuses on: analysis of the problem; specification of the model; running the model on the computer; comparison of predictions against data; modification of the model and a final justification and explanation of the end result. It does not focus on hard mathematical technique. Use of computer simulations is not yet a skill which needs to be assessed, according to the National Criteria; the following newspaper extracts describe an important everyday problem which could be modelled mathematically, to some effect.

Prof predicts killer disease explosion

By the turn of the century as many as 48,000 Britons could be dying of Aids each year... And by then the disease may have claimed the lives of 300,000 people. These shock claims came from an Edinburgh professor who has carried out research on the killer disease.

Professor Wilkie told the Sunday Post, 'My survey will help determine future insurance premium levels... The extra payouts caused by Aids deaths are already cutting bonuses. That won't be allowed to continue... blood tests for certain groups appear to be overdue'.

From The Sunday Post, 30 August, 1987

Aids hits more heterosexuals

Another 56 people developed Aids last month and 19 died of the disease, according to Department of Health figures released yesterday. The UK total since the epidemic began is 1,123 cases, of whom 624 have died. The disease is spreading among heterosexuals. Five cases attributed solely to heterosexual sex were reported last month... – bringing the total to 25 men and 17 women, including 19 who have died.

Six more haemophiliacs, a baby girl, and one more female drug addict developed Aids last month, but most of the 43 new cases were homosexuals and bisexuals. Nearly 1,000 gay men have developed the disease, and more than half of them have died.

From The Guardian, 10 November, 1987

These extracts illustrate the use of mathematics in modelling and in decision making. The accuracy of the extrapolated data is impressive – but probably spurious. These starting points could be used for student modelling of the epidemic (very hard without computer simulation); as a setting for discussions about exponential growth; problems of data gathering; assumptions made when modelling (e.g. how can a model account for the datum that no lesbians have yet died in the U.K. from Aids?); and the relationship between predictions and policy (e.g. compulsory screening; insurance premiums; HIV positive doctors continuing to practice; provision of free syringes to drug addicts...) These examples illustrate the dizzy heights (or perhaps the depths) to which practical mathematics can scale (or plunge). At present, we are all exploring the foothills and valleys.

There is little or no expertise to call upon in the general area of mathematical modelling, although the work of the Spode Group offers some useful starting points. More curriculum materials are urgently needed if practical mathematics is to fulfil some of its promises. The following list of contexts offers some starting points for explorations of everyday mathematics; of course, ideas need a great deal of careful development before they become useful and acceptable examination questions or foci for practical work or project work.

SEX: contraceptive reliability; dangers associated with long-term use of 'the pill'; risks of cervical cancer as a function of the number of sexual partners; the spread of Aids in homosexual and heterosexual populations (and the rate of spread as a function of the average number of sexual partners per year).

DRUGS: drinking and driving: is alcohol 'safer' than cannabis? Smoking or health (perhaps reviewing the specious arguments from tobacco companies between 1954 and 1980); addiction; dosage rates to maintain given levels of antibiotics in the bloodstream.

VIOLENCE: road traffic accidents (who is killed; at what time of the day; where; which vehicles are involved most); epidemiology of crime; major causes of death in different age groups; famine relief (how much is spent; does it just make things worse for later?); arms spending (e.g. Nato versus Warsaw Pact countries).

UNEMPLOYMENT: how would you calculate the number of people unemployed? Where do they live? If you were unemployed, where would be the best place to live? Which jobs are best paid? Do different kinds of training (YTS, A-levels, etc.) have different effects on your chances of getting a job? What should the Unemployment Benefit be?

HEALTH: is the NHS being starved of funds? How big will the population of over 80-year-olds be in the year 2000? Diet and health; is it worthwhile screening for: breast cancer; T.B....? What should be the balance of spending between preventative medicine (community medicine; health visiting; screening...) and restorative medicine (hospitals)?

ENVIRONMENT: how safe are nuclear power stations or coal-fired power stations? What levels of pollution are acceptable? Should new houses be built in inner city areas or in the green belt? How should rates be assessed? How does the Common Agricultural Policy work?

EDUCATION: are teachers underpaid? Do comprehensive schools produce better results than Grammar or Secondary Modern schools? Are public schools better still? How much grant should a sixth former receive?

Generating ideas for development is easy, compared with the task of converting ideas into lesson plans, or assessment tasks. It is important, though, that a far wider range of contexts are considered than have been considered so far in traditional curricula.

BIAS IN MATHEMATICS

The demands in the National Criteria that pupils must demonstrate some understanding of the part mathematics plays in the world raises an important issue: politics and bias in education. One might argue that in mathematics, examples which can be considered to be politically sensitive should be rejected in order to avoid possible accusations of bias. Unfortunately, this dramatically reduces the range of topics which can be considered which are interesting to children. Things which are personally important are usually interesting; things which are personally important to a large number of people are usually a focus of political debate. If every topic which is politically sensitive is ignored, the chances of presenting relevant mathematics is reduced. More important than a reduction in topic choice is a rejection of educational responsibility. Many agencies (advertizers, consumer groups, politicians, government, pressure groups, industry...) present arguments based on quasi-rational argument, supported by evidence of one sort or another, (often involving data collection and display) with the intention of persuading the populace of veracity of their point of view. It is important to equip pupils with the ability to challenge the methods of data collection, ('2 out of 3 people prefer...', 'there have only been nine deaths attributable to...') data presentation and the logic of the argument. Things are far harder to do when the arguments are emotionally loaded – so pupils need more practice in such situations. If pupils are to use mathematics as a powerful tool to help them evaluate arguments, reason correctly and make important personal decisions, they need practice at seeing biased communications for what they are and challenging data produced and conclusions drawn from these data. These skills need to be practised in contexts which are personally relevant: these are likely to be emotionally toned and politically sensitive. Such ideas depart a good deal from current practices in mathematics and great care will be needed in phasing them into the mainstream of mathematics. Nevertheless, if mathematics is to become a 'powerful tool' for pupils, they need to explore mathematics in contexts other than shopping, mortgages and planning trips. An important task will be to justify the use of interesting context to pupils and parents (and local politicians). Examples of the sorts of skills being rewarded by marking schemes (i.e. careful evaluation of evidence, rather than naive acceptance) should defuse qualms that mathematics is being taken over by people of one political persuasion or another. Worries have also been expressed over images projected about the relevance of mathematics for males and females. Attempts have been made to redress the marked imbalance in the names of males and females used in examination questions and to present both sexes equally in 'active' roles. Concerns about whether the topics chosen are inherently more interesting to boys than girls are harder to respond to. Questions on male-orientated topics are easily brought to mind: sports questions based on football, mechanics questions based on gunnery, aeroplanes dropping bombs on ships and probability questions based on gambling, implicitly suggest that mathematics is primarily of interest to males and is an exclusively suitable tool for solving problems in male dominated domains.

Working together on practical mathematics

The SEC has funded a project on the development and assessment of practical tasks in mathematics which can be taught and assessed within the GCSE framework whose aims are to provide information and resources for examining groups and teachers who face the challenge of assessing practical skills in mathematics by 1989. The project is directed for the Northern Examining Association (NEA) by the JMB in association with the SCME.

AMA—L

Hopefully, this project will produce a collection of exemplar tasks which are suitable for use in classrooms both to stimulate and assess practical mathematics. A collection of tasks, associated with marking schemes and suggestions for lesson plans is an essential starting point; however, each individual and each mathematics department will need to develop skills associated with practical work. The practices of the APU provide some important lessons:

- teachers need to experience practical mathematics themselves;
- departments need to discuss the pupil skills to be fostered and the ways they are to be assessed, by carrying out marking exercises together and by watching each other teach and assess. If this is not possible, then viewing videotapes together can provide a useful substitute activity;
- interviews with pupils need a teacher script; even if pupil attainment is not being marked, it is worthwhile having a list of skills which are to be encouraged, so that discussions with pupils about their progress have a firm behavioural base ('you need to cut out more accurately'; 'your explanation was wonderfully lucid'; 'try to sketch out a few different models before you do a lot of work on any particular one');
- sharing classroom experiences based on common tasks and inventing tasks together, both foster skill development.

Postcript

And now, a final problem in practical mathematics. You may think it is 'curious' or 'educational'; it isn't 'believable' but it might be an 'action' problem.

It is the year 2000. King's CSMS project has just published a final report, so that now almost all pupil misconceptions in mathematics are known about and can be remediated. The SEC (State Examination Committee) has published an interactive videodisk of examination tasks for practical skills which complement the ones on investigations, problem solving, groupwork, discussion and imitative skills. The Universal Oil Network for Mathematical Education has announced the Chartreuse Box on calculus for low attainers and so lesson plans are now available across all abilities for the entire curriculum, 5-18. The Gigantic Observation Schedule has been available for 3 years. A probationary teacher asks you how she shall use these resources.

Write your reply below. Justify your answer and show all your working.

As an extension, collect a few scripts from colleagues and work together to devise a marking scheme.

10 Approaching Assessment in Class

The last section examined a range of approaches intended to develop and assess 'missing activities' such as practical work, problem solving, groupwork and investigations. Faced with a plethora of new demands, it is essential for each teacher and each mathematics department to develop a coherent plan for teaching and assessment. Such plans cannot and should not, be imposed from outside; they must be based on internal discussions amongst colleagues. Everyone engaged in a new activity is likely to have something valuable to contribute. First attempts are likely to need revision; collaboration and the sharing of experiences, are all important to this learning process. A focusing question can help initiate the process:

'Are the objectives agreed by the mathematics department being met by current teaching practices?'

This is a broad question which requires a group discussion about the aims and objectives of mathematical education. These might be further analysed as follows:

- What are the aims and objectives of the department? (Will the lists in the National Criteria serve as a useful starting point?)
- What are current practices with regard to assessment and classroom practice? How are these assessments used?
- Is a wide enough range of assessment tasks being given to allow assessments to be made about general problem solving strategies such as the ability to try simple cases, or to generalize one's results?
- Is a wide enough range of assessment methods being used to describe social skills relevant to mathematical development on activities such as groupwork and discussion?

- Have pupils developed sufficient skill with regard to technologies such as calculators and computers?
- How might current aims and objectives be translated into descriptions of tasks which pupils should be able to perform?
- How can they be translated into descriptions of classroom activities?
- How do pupils view the new kinds of assessment being made?
- Do parents understand new forms of assessment?
- Are new kinds of assessment acceptable to every member of the mathematics department?
- What detrimental effects are likely to be introduced along with new forms of assessment? Can they be circumvented?
- Can a system be introduced whereby everyone in the department meets regularly to share experiences and to review and revise current practice (e.g. is the original list of aims and objectives in need of revision)?
- How can the departmental objectives be reconciled with the external demands of GCSE?
- How can the departmental objectives be reconciled with the National Curriculum?

Relating tests to objectives

A straightforward starting point is to ask each member of the department to examine a current test (end of term test; sample GCSE examination paper) and to judge the extent to which each question assesses each of the department's assessment objectives. In Table 10.2, numbers 3.1 to 3.17 refer to the assessment objectives set out in the National Criteria. A coding system like the one in Table 10.1 is appropriate for this task.

Table 10.1: Coding system

code	question relevance to the objective
O	irrelevant
ε	some small relevance
√	directly relevant
1	exclusively concerned with

Table 10.2:   A Checklist for Mathematical Objectives

Please complete the checklist showing which of the objectives 3.1–3.17 you consider to be met by each question.

Question	Objectives																
	3.1	3.2	3.3	3.4	3.5	3.6	3.7	3.8	3.9	3.10	3.11	3.12	3.13	3.14	3.15	3.16	3.17
A																	
B																	
C																	
D																	
E																	
F																	
G																	

Discussion of different people's codes will highlight different judgements about questions, and different interpretations of what each objective actually means.

A second outcome is likely to be that gaps are noticed (denoted by '⊙' and 'ε') in objectives asociated with everyday mathematics, tackling unstructured problems and others. An important task is to try to design questions which fill some of these gaps.

Of course other analyses of questions are possible. One could construct a test blueprint like the one described in the earlier chapter on *The Design and Evaluation of Standardized Tests* whose rows refer to process skills and whose columns refer to mathematical domains. Items can then be located within cells. Again, the purpose of the acitivity is to stimulate discussion about what people mean by different verbal labels, to identify gaps, and to design new questions to fill these gaps.

Learning how to teach for new assessment objectives is a challenge for almost everyone in mathematical education. There are a large number of publications to help this process available from the Mathematical Association, The Association of Teachers of Mathematics, the Open University and others. Individual staff members can be encouraged to try out different materials in their own classrooms and to share their experiences with others. Particular responsibilities might be delegated to each staff member, such as 'help everyone to get more groupwork going', 'set up some assessment tasks for practical mathematics', 'develop a plan to stimulate problem solving', and so on.

Monitoring the balance of classroom activities

Paragraph 243 of the Cockcroft Report asserted that mathematics teaching at all levels should involve: exposition; discussion between teacher and pupils; discussion between pupils; appropriate practical work; consolidation and practice of fundamental skills and routines; problem solving; applicable mathematics; and investigational work. The HMI Secondary Survey revealed a dominance of teacher exposition and of consolidation and practice by pupils, with rather little classroom time being devoted to any of the other activities. One can observe one's own allocation of time to different styles of teaching by keeping a checklist; a simple example is shown in Table 10.3.

An analysis of the structure of a particular lesson can be built up by noting class activities at regular intervals – say, every five minutes of the lesson. It is quite common for lessons to begin and end with exposition – for scene setting at the start, and to review progress at

Table 10.3: Allocation of time to different styles of teaching

exposition	: : : : : : : : : : :
discussion: teacher–pupils	: : : : : : : : : : :
discussion: pupil–pupil	: : : : : : : : : : :
practical work	: : : : : : : : : : :
consolidation	: : : : : : : : : : :
problem solving	: : : : : : : : : : :
applicable mathematics	: : : : : : : : : : :
investigational work	: : : : : : : : : : :

the end – even in lessons in which groupwork predominates. It is helpful to share lesson observation with a colleague so that a more accurate picture of time allocation emerges, to avoid distorting one's style because of the need to keep records, and to provide the basis for discussion about the balance of classroom activities and how they might be shaped. An alternative to regular sampling during a lesson is a description from memory of the time allocated to different activities. This is likely to produce rather unreliable results, although records collected over several lessons can still prove useful.

The use of such records, however collected, is simple and obvious. Examination of the balance of classroom activities over a period of time is likely to highlight gaps in the experiences which pupils receive, which one can attempt to remediate. Certain styles of teaching may be unfamiliar; colleagues can be a useful source of advice about how one might proceed, as can direct observation of their lessons. A number of helpful teaching resources are referred to at the end of this volume.

Pupil conceptions of assessment

Pupil conceptions of the purposes of testing are important. If pupils feel that mathematical education is something which is being imposed upon them as opposed to something in which they actively participate, then their views of testing and assessment in general are likely to be somewhat negative. If assessment is viewed as something which is done for someone else's benefit – for example, to put pupils in rank order for streaming in school, or for determining likely job prospects, a high degree of anxiety about the whole testing enterprise is a reasonable response. If pupils feel that the tests are for *their* benefit then test anxieties are likely to be reduced.

It is well worthwhile talking to pupils about their own views of assessment and asking how particular abilities can best be assessed. This can provide interesting insights into the way pupils view the whole assessment process. The importance of a dialogue with pupils about the nature and use of assessment can hardly be over emphasized. Discussion about assessment offers a way to foster pupil reflection about the nature of the mathematical enterprise. Asking pupils to think about assessment requires them to think about those aspects of mathematics which are valuable; the ways they can be displayed and assessed and the uses to which such assessments can be put.

Observe what happens when work is handed back which has been both annotated with comments and graded. Do pupils spend time reading comments in detail and thinking about them, or do they turn straight to the grade and talk about relative achievements with their friends? When pupils see the value of assessment as a formative process written comments and discussions are likely to help their mathematical development a good deal; until then, they are unlikely to be useful.

One of the current major tasks in mathematical education is to devise assessment schemes which sample reasonable symptoms of the sorts of attainment defined to be desirable. Pupils themselves will be aware of paradoxes such as:

– real world tasks that are rarely relevant to pupil needs;
– practical tasks that have no practical uses;
– groupwork that is assessed by a write-up of results without collaboration;
– investigational work assessed in conditions of timed examinations.

Discussions with parents

A number of schools have arranged parents' evenings where parents are invited along to learn about changes in the teaching and assessment of mathematics brought about by GCSE. Changes from past practices can be explained; justifications abound in the *Cockcroft Report, Mathematics 5 to 16* and elsewhere. One activity for such meetings is to offer a page of GCE and CSE questions, together with a page of GCSE questions and to ask for comments about which set would be more useful to have mastered, which set would be more enjoyable to do. Discussions about changes in teaching style can follow on from this task analysis.

Reconciling external demands and internal desires

How much teacher autonomy is desirable in pupil accreditation? One might argue that teachers (and pupils) are best able to make judgements about pupil attainment; and they are best able to devise assessment tasks suited to the educational experience of their classes. Set against this argument is the problem of moderation. If outside agencies are to make judgements about the relative merits of pupils from different schools then some basis for comparison is needed. If all coursework is set and assessed by teachers without regard to the problems of moderation, their assessments are likely to be of little use for predicting performance in further education or employment. If teacher assessments are found to be poor predictors, they are likely to be little used; absence of use will lead to devaluation of teacher assessments and if such assessments are the only basis by which coursework is judged, then coursework itself will become devalued as an assessment tool. This is likely to have the undesirable effect that only externally moderated, timed, written forms of assessment will be valued and these will again become the major inspiration for classroom practice.

Absence of teacher autonomy is likely to have as negative an impact on school life as has the absence of pupil autonomy. Externally imposed timed written examinations seemed to have had this effect in the past; if coursework and assessment of practical tasks and investigations are all set and assessed externally, an undesirable state of affairs is likely to continue. So a tension exists between the desire for some measure of relative performance between pupils in different classes, and the need for teacher autonomy in the setting and assessment of examination tasks. An obvious way to resolve the conflict is provided by teacher moderation groups where groups of teachers within the same school and in consortia of local school, meet and discuss educational goals, methods of assessment and assessment tasks. These consortia then moderate each other's work. The benefits of such a scheme are that a great deal of teacher involvement is guaranteed; teachers are free – subject to persuading their professional colleagues – to assess coursework elements in whatever way they see fit. Everyone has a vested interest in fostering autonomy in the classroom and everyone has a vested interest in ensuring some comparability in assessment methods across different schools.

Coursework moderation also provides the opportunity for teachers to meet to discuss classroom practices and methods of assessment. The creation of self-help groups where ideas are shared is important. It is hard to improve one's own performance without contact with professional colleagues who can act both as a source of new ideas and as a competent audience to listen to one's own ideas with a constructively critical ear. An essential purpose of meetings between teachers is to increase the group's commitment to self-education. Classroom experiences with new forms of assessment can be shared; this is particularly valuable in new domains such as assessing oral mathematics and practical mathematics, or the conduct of mathematical investigations.

The advocacy of teacher involvement in the design of assessment procedures is an attempt to foster teacher autonomy and reflection about the nature of such activities. Earlier arguments for pupil involvement in assessment activities are also based on the need to bring about pupil reflection about the nature of such activities. It is important that any model for the development of mathematical education should reveal such essential similarities. Models of problem solving should apply to the problem solving of teachers as well as to the problem solving of children. There should be some similarities between the models of problem solving advocated for pure mathematical investigation and for the models of problem solving advocated for facing challenges such as 'how do we introduce practical skills into mathematics?'. Similarly, as teachers are encouraged to explore new methods of assessment and classroom practice in an attempt to improve their personal skills, it is important to ask *pupils* for feedback about the relative success of the new assessment processes and new classroom practices. A framework for discussing the acquisition of mathematical knowlege will be the focus of the next chapter.

11 Assessment, Teaching and Learning

For teachers, the kinds of assessment tasks which are set reflect judgements about the mathematical skills which are valued – pupil performance provides feedback about personal success in fostering such skills. For pupils, the tasks set and the classroom activities in which they engage shape their definitions of the nature of mathematics. Changing assessment tasks and the nature of the classroom activities which take place provides a shift of attention, and has the potential to bring about major reconceptualizations about the nature of mathematics, and mathematical education, for both pupils and teachers. Reflection about classroom practices and pupil performance is an essential element in learning more about one's self as a learner, a mathematician and a mathematical educator. A focus on assessment is critically important for this enhanced understanding. The acquisition of knowledge about mathematics is a cyclical process. Acquiring knowledge affects our ability to acquire more knowledge. Mathematical learning involves the active construction of knowledge; the way that new information is viewed depends on the knowledge which the learner already holds. These assertions apply to everyone engaged in mathematical education – pupils, teachers, examiners, and curriculum developers.

There is a body of research which sets out to explore pupil constructions about mathematics; but almost no work has been done on teacher constructs (or on curriculum developer or examiner constructs). Pupils have constructions about many aspects of their world. One can classify these constructs crudely into the domains of cognition (what does the pupil know and how is this knowledge arranged, represented etc.), social knowledge (knowledge and beliefs about groupwork, and other inter-personal relationships in class) and emotional responses (how the person feels about various aspects of mathematics).

Teachers have constructs which include their beliefs about pupil constructs. In addition they have detailed knowledge of the subject matter and beliefs about the relative importance of different aspects; they have theories about teaching, some of which can be stated explicitly and some of which are implicit, as theories-in-action about teaching.

Examiners and curriculum developers have constructs about teachers' beliefs, including constructs about teachers' knowledge and teachers' theories-in-action; constructs about pupils' cognitive, emotional and social states; and conceptions about teacher constructs concerning pupils constructs. In addition, of course, curriculum developers and examiners have their own knowledge and beliefs about mathematics – which skills are most valuable and how they can be assessed – and their own theories about teaching.

So every agent in mathematical education has an elaborate system of personal constructions about the nature of the enterprise, about the roles of each actor (pupil, teacher, examiner, curriculum developer) and their own inter-relations with these other actors.

If one is to change one's behaviour as a teacher it is necessary to change constructs and theories, as well as simply increasing one's repertoire of skills. It will probably prove harder to change teacher conceptions than to change those of pupils. Pupils have fewer, and weaker, constructs about the nature of the mathematical enterprise; they are likely to have little problem in adjusting to whatever new knowledge frameworks we choose to offer them. Teachers have far greater problems. The existence of extensive knowledge, and a particular view of mathematics makes it harder to adapt to change. New events are viewed through existing mental structures; a great danger is that genuinely innovatory ideas are assimilated to existing frameworks and distorted in the process. For example: 'Problem solving? Do it all the time. Try this one: if five men take six weeks to build a bridge...' illustrates the relabelling of old practices with new jargon, while changing nothing.

Learning about mathematical education

What sort of actions follow from the view that everyone constructs their knowledge? Two questions need to be addressed.

- How can new ideas be explained and understood by pupils and colleagues?
- How does one continue to learn?

Understanding and explaining new ideas

One way to explore pupil frameworks is to ask them to invent questions which will assess the ability of other pupils in particular intellectual domains. For example, in the area of number work, when pupils are set the task of deciding whether other pupils can choose operations appropriately, or understand place value in problems involving decimals, their questions offer ideas about the way pupils see problem difficulty. Similarly, a consideration of the tasks which other teachers set, or which appear on examination papers, give a view of implicit theories about what is important, and/or difficult in particular subject matter; discussion (or discussion documents) can extend this knowledge.

The National Criteria, syllabuses from examination boards, and exemplar questions, are essential in the process of trying to understand new curriculum intentions. Straightforward changes of content are easy to specify and understand. However, not all changes in assessment practice are easy to define; the mathematical education community is actively looking for ways to assess process skills, practical work, oral skills and the like. Exemplars of relevant tasks, which are essential to those trying to understand what is meant by the verbal descriptions, are lacking. Explicit task definitions, and clear descriptions of appropriate pupil behaviour are urgently needed. A great virtue of both examination questions with scripts and marking schemes, and detailed observation schedules, is the role they have to play in understanding the constructs of others, and in negotiating definitions. Complete and detailed descriptions of new methods of assessment define the relative importance of new skills in the overall scheme; observation schedules have a parallel role to play in understanding the processes to be fostered.

Continuing to learn

There has been a good deal of research effort which sets out to change pupils' conceptual frameworks. What does this work teach students of mathematical education about their own knowledge? The main thrust of such studies is usually to elicit pupils' conceptions about some mathematical topic, and then to provide learning opportunities in which pupils encounter situations which disconfirm their views. What are analogous activities for teachers? It is relatively easy to teach mathematics and set assessment tasks in a style which is consistent with one's existing conceptual frameworks;

rather more difficult to explore situations which might challenge these frameworks, or indeed one's whole world view about the nature of the educational process. To do so requires a focus on new aspects of mathematical attainment and some practice at new methods of teaching and learning.

One begins by describing clearly one's personal constructions about significant events, then conducts studies and investigations to explore them. The information received from these studies feeds back to enrich existing conceptions, and from time to time, might even revolutionize them. A question to be asked repeatedly of current beliefs and practices is: 'what evidence would convince me that I am wrong?'. One should then make sure that such evidence is sought out, and evaluated carefully.

The way that attention is directed either by one's self or by others has the potential to shape beliefs about the nature of doing and learning mathematics. A major role played by timed, written examinations has been to focus attention quite disproportionately on those aspects of mathematics which can be tackled via such assessment processes. Consequently a great deal of current mathematical education is directed towards a rather narrow range of goals, with direct implications for beliefs about the nature of mathematics. Similarly knowledge and expertise in different aspects of teaching reflects pressures to present a somewhat restricted range of classroom activities and experiences for pupils than one might wish.

Pressures towards narrowing, even if they have not led to a narrowing of beliefs about the essential nature of mathematics, are likely to have restricted domains of expertise in teaching. New challenges posed by GCSE offer the chance to revert to wider views of the nature of mathematical activity, and to extend personal competence in a wider variety of teaching situations. It is clear that one cannot expect one's expertise in such matters as fostering problem solving, stimulating investigations, and facilitating fruitful groupwork to emerge fully fledged, and at a comparable level to skills in fostering pupil's mathematical technique, without practice. A good deal of active learning will be required. The challenges posed by GCSE should be viewed as potential providers of rich learning experiences for everyone involved in mathematical education. Teachers are now being induced to attend to rather different aspects of pupil performance than have been attended to before. Knowledge in detecting different kinds of mathematical attainment, and in adjusting actions to stimulate different kinds of mathematical learning will improve with experience.

Revisions of one's knowledge and skill can only be done by one's self; others might help with the process, for example by discussing appropriate methods one might use to shape behaviour, but other people cannot pass their knowledge on directly. Clear articulation of one's goals, exemplified by task descriptions and marking schemes, and clear descriptions of desirable classroom behaviours are essential to this process. They must be associated with systematic attempts to modify one's behaviour and periods of reflection on success and failure.

Review

This volume has emphasized the centrality of assessment to the whole endeavour of mathematical education, and the intimate association between assessment, teaching and learning. Our implicit goals as educators are reflected in the assessment tasks we set to pupils. The tasks which pupils face, together with their classroom experiences define for them the nature of the mathematical enterprise.

Everyone concerned with mathematical education has a responsibility to improve the range and nature of the tasks which are used to assess mathematical attainment. I hope that this volume helps in this process.

Appendix 1: Summary of features of GCSE syllabuses*:

Examining Group	NEA	MEG (Schemes I, II & SMP)	MEG (SMP 11-16)	SEG	LEAG	WJEC	NISEC
Levels of entry	P Q R	Foundation Intermediate Higher	Foundation Intermediate Higher	1 2 3	X Y Z	1 2 3	Basic Intermediate High
Range of grades (targets in italics)	P-*EFG* Q-*CDEF*(G)* R-*ABCD* (EFG)*	F-*EFG* I-*CDEF* H-*ABCD*	F-(D) *EFG** I-*CDE*(F)* H-*ABC*(D)*	1-*EFG* 2-*CDEF* 3-*ABCD*	X-*EFG* Y-*CDEF* Z-*ABCD*	1-*EFG* 2-*CDEF* 3-*ABCD*	B-*EFG* I-*CDEF* H-*ABCD*
mental/ aural test				Aural tests to mirror each written paper – 10 per cent of marks		Aural tests included in assessment scheme for Practical Mathematics.	Aural and computation test set at each level (half an hour, 10 per cent)

* Parentheses indicate exceptional awards

* Parentheses indicate exceptional awards

AMA—M

Without centre-based assessment

	NEA Syllabus A Scheme I and Syllabus B Scheme I	MEG Scheme I	MEG SMP	SEG	LEAG Syllabus A SMP	WJEC Scheme B	NISEC Syllabus B
Written papers	1 2 3 4	F I H 1 2 3 + + + 4 5 6	1 2 3 4	1 2 3 4	1 2 3 4	1 2 3 4	B I H I III V + + + II IV VI
Time (hours)	1½ 1½ 2 2½	1½ 2 2 1½ 2 2½	1½ 2 2 2½	1½ 1½ 2 2	Syllabus A 1½ 1½ 2¼ 2½ SMP 1½ 1½ 2 2½	1½ 2 2½ 2½	1½ 2 2½ 1½ 2 2½
Percentage marks	P 50 50 Q 45 55 R 45 55	50 50 50 50 50 50	F 50 50 I 50 50 H 50 50	145 45 2 45 45 3 45 45	X 50 50 Y 50 50 Z 50 50	150 50 2 50 50 3 50 50	45 45 45 45 45 45

With centre-based assessment

	NEA Syllabus A, Scheme II, Syllabus B, Scheme II	MEG Scheme II	MEG SMP 11–16	SEG	LEAG Syllabus B	WJEC Scheme A	NISEC Syllabus A
Written papers	Identical papers P 37½ 37½ 42 Q 33 42 R 33	Section B of second paper omitted F I H 1½ 2 2 ¾ 1 1¼ 50 50 50 25 25 25	1 2 3 4 1½ 2 2½ 2½ hours F 35 35 I 35 35 H 35 35	Different papers 1 2 3 4 1 1½ 2 25 25 25 25 25 25	Reduction of Syllabus A papers	Identical papers	Identical papers
Percentage of marks allocated to centre-based element	25 per cent	25 per cent	25 per cent coursework and 5 per cent oral	40 per cent	25 per cent coursework	c. 25 per cent (to include aural test)	20 per cent
Number of pieces of work	not specified	5	8 (6 in 1988 only)	Three units. Each unit to be a single task or series of short tasks. One unit to be an extended task.	5 (≥ 1 from each category) (≤ 2 per category)	2 (+ 3 exercises for Level 1)	4 assignments
Topics set by Group/chosen by centre	Chosen by centre	Chosen by centre: categories specified	Set by group	Chosen by centre	Set by group or centre's own tasks	Set by group or centre's own topics	Chosen by centre: categories suggested
Set at level/determined by outcome	By outcome	By outcome	Set at levels (Some two levels, some all levels)	By outcome	First 3 appropriate for all levels: last 2 set at levels X/Y or Y/Z	Set at levels 2/3 or 1	

	NEA Syllabus A Scheme II Syllabus B Scheme II	MEG Scheme II	MEG SMP 11-16	SEG	LEAG Syllabus B	WJEC Scheme A	NISEC Syllabus A
Categories of coursework tasks	Not specified	1. Practical geometry 2. An everyday application of Mathematics 3. Statistics and/or probability 4. An investigation 5. A centre-approved topic	1. Investigational and practical tasks; 6 skills specified 2. More substantial tasks	One extended unit. Other units are single tasks or collections of assignments	1. Pure investigations 2. Problems 3. Practical work	*Level 1* Investigations Practical skills *Level 2/3* Practical investigations Problem solving	1. Practical geometry/ measurement/ Everyday application of Maths/Statistics 2. Pure mathematics investigation
Timing	Not specified. Integral part of study in final two years of course	At least two in final 12 months of course	For 1989 and after—during the first four terms in the final two years	Any time during five terms prior to examination		Any time during two years prior to examination	Any time during two years prior to examination
Oral component	Given as, possibly, record of course-work	Given as possible controlled element of coursework in form of tape-recorded exchange between teacher and pupil	Two oral tests – mirror of written levels. Group to provide item banks of questions and mark schemes	ORAL Series of discussions about candidates work	Mental test at each level 5 per cent		Discussions to take place as part of development of coursework
Additional conditions	1. Nature and organization not specified – but not series of written tests 2. Some must be extended 3. Sufficient supervision to assure authenticity of work	1. Each assignment must contain an element carried out under controlled conditions. 2. Suggested time for each assignments is 2–3 weeks	Tasks belong to one of three categories: ST–at school with time limit of one hour, supervised S –at school, supervised H –out of school	1. Units to be an integral part of course. 2. Units to meet syllabus specifications. 3. Stages of units specified 4. One unit must be an extended piece of work.	$\frac{25}{120}$ of marks available for units must be assigned to oral assessment	Suggested time – two sessions per week over two 4-week periods	At least one assignment from each of the two specified categories
Assessment	Guidelines for award of marks provided	Scheme of assessment provided	Scheme of marking provided	Marking criteria provided	Marking scheme provided	Marking scheme provided	Teachers attend Board training session. Marking scheme provided
Moderation	Statistical screening	Postal inspection	Moderator	Consensus	Assessor	Inspection	Moderator

References

ASSESSMENT OF PERFORMANCE UNIT (1980–2). *Mathematical Development:* Primary Surveys 1 and 2, Secondary Surveys 1, 2 and 3. London: HMSO.

BELL, A. (1983). 'Diagnostic teaching – the design of teaching using research on understanding', *Zentralblatt für Didaktik der Mathematik*, 83, 2.

BELL, A., COSTELLO J., and KUCHEMANN, D. (1983). *A Review of Research in Mathematical Education, Part A: Learning and Teaching.* Windsor: NFER-NELSON.

BURKHARDT, H. (1981). *The Real World and Mathematics.* London: BLACKIE.

COCKCROFT REPORT. GREAT BRITAIN. DEPARTMENT OF EDUCATION AND SCIENCE. (1982). *Mathematics Counts.* London: HMSO.

COUNCIL FOR EDUCATIONAL TECHNOLOGY (1987). *Will Mathematics Count?* Hatfield: AUCBE.

CROWTHER REPORT. GREAT BRITAIN. DEPARTMENT OF EDUCATION AND SCIENCE (1959). *15 to 18: A Report of the Central Advisory Council for Education.* London: HMSO.

DEPARTMENT OF EDUCATION AND SCIENCE (1985). *GCSE: The National Criteria: Mathematics.* London: HMSO.

DEPARTMENT OF EDUCATION AND SCIENCE AND THE WELSH OFFICE (1987). *The National Curriculum 5–16 – a consultation document.* London. HMSO.

FOXMAN, D. (1985). 'Current practice in the assessment of low attainers, *T.E.S. Maths Extra,* May 10.

FOXMAN, D. (1987). *Assessing Practical Mathematics in Secondary Schools.* Windsor: NFER-NELSON.

HART, K. (1981). *Children's Understanding of Mathematics.* London: JOHN MURRAY.

HER MAJESTY'S INSPECTORATE OF SCHOOLS (1979). *Aspects of Secondary Education in England.* London: HMSO.

HER MAJESTY'S INSPECTORATE OF SCHOOLS (1985). *Mathematics from 5 to 16.* London: HMSO.

JOFFE, L. (1985). *Practical Testing in Mathematics at Age 15*. London: ASSESSMENT OF PERFORMANCE UNIT.

JOINT MATRICULATION BOARD/SHELL CENTRE FOR MATHEMATICAL EDUCATION (1984). *Problems With Patterns and Numbers: an O-level module*. Manchester: JOINT MATRICULATION BOARD.

JOINT MATRICULATION BOARD/SHELL CENTRE FOR MATHEMATICAL EDUCATION (1985). *The Language of Functions and Graphs: an examination module for secondary schools*. Manchester: JOINT MATRICULATION BOARD.

JOINT MATRICULATION BOARD/SHELL CENTRE FOR MATHEMATICAL EDUCATION (1987). *Assessment of Numeracy Through Problem Solving: Introduction to the scheme*. Manchester: JOINT MATRICULATION BOARD.

OGBORN, J. (1987). 'Computational modelling in science', In: LEWIS R. and TAGG, E.D. (Eds) *Trends in Computer Assisted Education*. London: BLACKWELL SCIENTIFIC PUBLICATIONS.

OPEN UNIVERSITY (1980). *Curriculum in Action: Practical Classroom Evaluation: P234*. Milton Keynes: OPEN UNIVERSITY PRESS.

RIDGWAY, J. (1987). 'Of course ICAI is impossible: worse though, it may be seditious'. In SELF, J. (Ed). *Intelligent Computer-Aided Instruction*. London: CHAPMAN AND HALL.

RIDGWAY, J. (1988a). *A Review of Mathematics Tests*. Windsor: NFER-NELSON.

RIDGWAY, J. (Ed) (1988b). *Observation Methods in Education*. London: CROOM-HELM.

SECONDARY EXAMINATIONS COUNCIL (1986). *Mathematics GCSE: A Guide for Teachers*. Milton Keynes: OPEN UNIVERSITY PRESS.

SEWELL, B. (1981). *Use of Mathematics in Everyday Life*. London: ADVISORY COUNCIL FOR ADULT AND CONTINUING EDUCATION.

Mathematics Teaching is published by the Association of Teachers of Mathematics, 7 Shaftsbury Street, Derby DE3 8YB.

The Mathematical Gazette is published by the Mathematical Association, 259 London Road, Leicester LE2 3BE.

Index